ISBN: 978-0-615-39914-0
Published by: Erotic Flow and PAR Intz.
San Francisco, CA
Cover and Book Design by David DeCitore
Cover Photograph by Ian Chin Photography
Cover Photoshop Work by C&E Imagination, Attero Media, & Adagio Digital
Erotic Flow Logo Design and Art by David DeCitore and Attero Media
Illustration Art by David DeCitore and Milan Vasev - eLance.com contractor.

Printed in the United States of America

Dedication

This book is dedicated to the beauty of women and the pleasuring of their mind, body, and soul. To couples and the new exciting experience and deep connection they will enjoy. To men and the happiness they will receive from a skill set that will reward them for the rest of their lives. Erotic sexuality is the art and passion of my soul. Thus, I want to inspire my readers to express their erotic souls and create experiences of unforgettable passion, sensuality, intimacy, and erotic ecstasy! Enjoy the book.

Erotic Flow

Erotic Flow (EF) was started to inspire lovers to seduce each other's mind, body, and soul. To help couples cultivate the art of creating sensual, passionate, and erotic experiences. EF provides the knowledge and tools to assist couples in expressing their erotic souls. EF specializes in devising creative erotic experiences. We aim to inspire people to fall in love with pleasuring their lover, creating erotic experiences, and flowing together.

"Erotic" is creative, sensual, and passionate sexual expression. "Flow" is two entities becoming one, sending each other erotic energy, and getting lost in the moment. Hence, Erotic Flow is creatively expressing the art of your erotic soul, combined with creating moments when you and your lover's passion, energy, and soul become one. Moments when you become lost in each other, when nothing else exists, except the intense, deep, and delicious connection with your lover.

EF is about giving pleasure with every cell in your body and having every ounce of your soul engulfed in the ecstasy of each other's chemistry, when you feel every kiss, lick, and suck coming from your entire body. It is stimulating the senses (what she/he sees, tastes, smells, hears, and feels) and ultimately seducing each other's mind, body, and soul.

Our products and services will contribute to creating this experience. Additionally, EroticFlow.com is designed to deliver a multimedia learning experience. It provides music, videos, products, services, social networking, consulting, and education to assist you in expressing your erotic soul. Learn more in the Resources section of this book.

How to Use

This Book

This book is designed to seduce a female reader, so she says YES, to trying anal sexuality, but it is written addressing the man because he is going to implement the instructions. The book is structured to progressively stimulate a woman through what she reads and sees. There are 76 instructional images to make the book easy and entertaining to learn from. The images were created with three goals in mind:

1. To illustrate what needs to happen and how.

2. To aid learning and make the illustrations entertaining by adding creative art. The more unique an image is, the more memorable it is.

3. To progressively increase stimulation. The images are drawn with a variety of sexy people, and the erotic images progressively increase in sexuality to arouse a reader visually as she/he consumes the mind candy of the book. There is corresponding text to every image, leading her imagination through fantasy, and there is dirty talk to add excitement.

Therefore, after a woman reads the book, the goal is for her to say to her man, "Babe, read this book, and let's do everything it says!" Read the testimonials in the book and check EroticFlow.com for new testimonials and video testimonials that might touch a personal cord with you.

The book has two purposes. First, to give couples a pleasurable step-by-step guide to enjoy anal sexuality in a painless manner. Second, to give women incredible, intense, and explosive orgasms! Many women do not know that they can have the most incredible orgasms of their lives through adding anal stimulation to their sexual repertoire. The reason she will feel incredible is because the techniques provide stimulation to multiple erogenous zones simultaneously. Some techniques pleasure her nipples, clitoris, G-Spot, U-Spot, pussy, and gem (her ass), all at the same time. When a woman experiences this arousal in conjunction with your passion, connection, and erotic energy, this typically leads to having explosive, full-body orgasms.

This book provides a solution to four types of situational scenarios. I will cover how to approach these scenarios.

Scenario 1: The man wants his woman to try anal sexuality, and she is also interested but wants to make sure the process does not hurt. This scenario is easy to address. If both are curious and interested, but the man is initiating the desire, the man should read the book first, then give it to his woman to read, so she knows what will happen, and then both should talk about it afterwards.

Together Strategy: Also, you two can read this book together, so you two can talk about it as you read it. If you read it together, the man can read it to his woman, and whenever I state "you will," he could read out loud "I will" and lead her through a fantasy. Read it all the way through and, before every night of the 7 Nights to Ecstasy System, re-read the content for that night and then implement it, so the instructions are fresh in your mind. What should women do? It would be good for the woman to read the night's content beforehand, too, so she knows what is supposed to happen and can help guide her man in case he forgets something. She should just relax and enjoy. Some books state that the woman can do techniques to help relax her muscles with deep breathing. Well, that might be necessary when a guy is trying to have anal sex in one night or two. That is not going to happen in this system. All a woman has to do is enjoy the new arousal of her body.

Scenario 2: The woman is interested in anal sexuality and wants her man to try it with her. She can read the book first and then give it to her man to read, specifying what she wants to experience most. Then both do the Together Strategy stated above.

Scenario 3: The man wants his woman to try anal sexuality, but she is not interested for a wide variety of reasons or is extremely against it. This happens often, and I have run into this challenge many times. It is one of the main reasons I wrote this book. Everything from very scared of pain, not clean, guy is too big, religion, etc. Most guys think they can talk a woman into doing it. NOT! That is not going to work. The main reason this book will work to overcome that challenge is because of its philosophy. This book is not about getting a woman to have anal sex; you have to throw away all self-motivated intentions. The only way it works is if you genuinely enter this journey with the sole purpose of GIVING PLEASURE to your woman. Yes, it is all about giving her pleasure, falling in love with the pleasuring of her heart, mind, body, and soul. With this pure intention, she will be able to experience arousal at a pace that gives her immense stimulation and, most importantly, builds trust.

Most of the advice out there assumes that you can do this in one or two nights. Not for most women! Just put yourself in their shoes and think how you would want things to happen. Since talking is not the answer, the method in this book is designed to seduce her body with a variety of small, exciting steps of pleasure, letting her enjoy every step of the way, so she yearns eagerly for the next step.

First, commit to reading this book in detail; do not skip steps or go fast through them. Do the small steps to pleasure her body. Promise yourself that you are only going to go as far as she is comfortable experiencing pleasure, and you will see that your patience will lead to lots of pleasure. Even if it takes longer for your woman than the 7 Nights to Ecstasy System because of her personal evolution, just lose yourself in those moments of pleasuring her and flow in those moments, by which I mean nothing else exists—just you and her, and your connection. If all your energy and soul is engulfed in every kiss, lick, suck, and caress, you will eventually progress further and further. Through flowing together and building trust in your intentions, she will experience immense pleasure from anal sexuality.

So, here is an approach that you can take for Scenario 3. Implement Night 1 without talking about it; just implement the instructions and see how she enjoys the stimulation you are giving her. If she likes it, then do the same for Night 2. Buy the tools needed for Night 3 and have them ready. If she has enjoyed Nights 1 and 2, she will probably enjoy experiencing Night 3's activities. At this point you can introduce this book to her so she can read the pleasure she will enjoy and so she can clean accordingly for the upcoming nights.

Implement Night 3 and see how she likes the activities. Afterwards, ask what she liked and what she might want you to modify. Set up for

Night 4 and implement the instructions. When you talk now, talk about what she enjoyed, not about trying to convince her of doing more. Just keep genuinely building on the pleasure you are giving her body, her mind, and your connection. She then will yearn for more and more. Keep progressing until you complete the 7 Nights.

If it takes longer for your woman, that is fine. It does not matter how long it takes for your specific situation, because you two are enjoying new excitement and fulfillment. When she feels and knows that time does not matter, things will progress. Remember, your genuine intention is to make her feel really, really, really good and create incredible moments together. You will go only as far as she continues to enjoy it, so the responsibility is on you to make her feel incredible! If a man falls in love with pleasuring his woman, so that she feels that every lick, suck, kiss, and caress is coming from his heart and soul, he will make her heart, mind, body, and soul feel amazing!

Scenario 4: The woman is interested, but her man is not for a variety of reasons. Does this actually happen? That is what I thought when I wrote this scenario, but surprising to me, it does. I met a guy who felt like this. What changed his mind was finding out that he could give his woman the most incredible orgasms she has ever experienced. He wanted to be the one to do that for her, and he wanted to have that skill-set forever! So communicate that benefit to him, and you will arouse his interest.

Read more on assessing your individual situation in section 2.5 "Assess how she feels about anal play, so you can design the process exactly for her." Erotic dialogue is used to explain the system and techniques. Read "Erotic Dialogue" in the Resouces section for the reasons the current terms are used. This book has the views of women built into the instructions, women who have gone through the system and 7 female book editors have contributed to the book. Also, in the Resources section, learn how to provide your feedback and get rewarded for it. Check EroticFlow.com for more facts on anal sexuality, erotic music, and a Q&A. Some women have stated that they need to see for themselves that anal sexuality is pleasurable to believe it. Therefore, the members section of the site provides links to videos of women having orgasms from anal sexuality and hot anal sex. The site will continue to provide more resources to benefit people, including a blog and starter kits. With this book, other EF products, and the website, you have the tools you need to thoroughly and passionately Arouse Her Anal Ecstasy. Enjoy your journey!

Testimonials

Ladies, in an effort to expand the variety in our bedroom, my boyfriend and I read Arouse Her Anal Ecstasy. *My man has always longed to add anal pleasure to our sex lives, but due to a painful experience in my past, I wrote off anal sex, and judged that it was not for me. We implemented the highly pleasurable and easy techniques, and in time I was experiencing mind-blowing orgasms from clitoral and vaginal stimulation and anal penetration simultaneously!!! My boyfriend is well endowed, and I was skeptical in the beginning, fearing that it might hurt, but it did not. Your man will learn just how to get you relaxed, excited, and eager for this erotic treat!!*

Mariana L.

When I first tried anal a long time ago with a boyfriend, it was SO painful, and I swore I would never try it again. But then I read "The Book" with my boyfriend, and we tried it, and it was amazing! We went really slowly and gradually at first, just like the book suggests, and it didn't hurt. Instead, it felt really good. And over time, I wanted that more than regular sex because it felt so good. I think one thing I didn't understand about anal was that you can still have face-to-face sex, so it can still be intimate and incredibly sexy at the same time.

And doing anal this way, it was easy to stimulate my clitoris at the same time, either by him or with a toy, an incredible combination. I can't say enough about how grateful I am that we learned this technique for anal, and now it's part of our regular sexual repertoire. Oh yeah, and my boyfriend is pretty incredibly happy with it, too. A huge thank you from him!

Lisa T.

The techniques taught in this book are unlike anything that I have ever read before, and it works! I had tried anal sex before, and it hurt going in, going out, and during the entire ordeal. I thought it was simply that I didn't like anal sex, but after understanding that there was a correct method, it completely transformed my sex life. After studying these techniques there was absolutely no discomfort in the beginning, which was surprising because he is more endowed than any previous partner I've had. The first time my boyfriend tried it, I didn't believe that he was inside my anus. I had him take a picture to show me! No pain at all, only pleasure.

Once it was inside, along with some other playful techniques mentioned in the book, I was able to have the most intense orgasm of my life ... and that is not an exaggeration. What I enjoy most about this method is that it doesn't require a big change in my sex life; it complements what I am already doing, with great, easy suggestions. I don't know about you, but my mom didn't teach me about anal sex, so having this book is useful and has added an amazing layer of sensuality that I wasn't aware of. My boyfriend loves it, and I am grateful for it.

Cynthia G.

Ouch!!! That was what I associated with "anal sex." I had only experienced pain and discomfort when it came to anal sex in my 10 years of sexual history. It had been my experience that every male I encountered had the one fantasy of anal sex and had no clue what it entailed. Anal sex had been introduced to me by several partners and had left me running for the door. I never in my life believed that I could receive any type of pleasure out of anal sex. I simply wanted to do it to please my partner. I researched many times how to go about it in the most painless way and had found little or nothing on this topic, which was displayed as pleasurable and painless in every porn video created. It wasn't until my boyfriend implemented the techniques in this book and took his time to introduce me to anal sex in a sensual way through this methodical process, that I not only was comfortable with anal sex but found it pleasurable. After my first full penetration session, there was no turning back. I wanted to replay the intense orgasm that I had received through anal sex over and over. The methods and process in this book will change your sexual experience when it comes to becoming aroused by anal sex and obtaining an orgasm. It will give you an out-of-body, intimate experience with your partner that I guarantee you have never experienced!

Jennifer M.

Arouse Her Anal Ecstasy

Table of Contents

Chapter Three ~ Prepare for Pleasure ~

Making Anal Play Good, Clean, Fun 36

Chapter Four ~ Seduction Philosophy~

Enjoy the Process of Pleasuring Her and Give Her Thrilling Orgasms Every Little Step of the Way 58

Chapter Five ~ Erotic Anal Play ~

Chapter One

Introduction

The Unique Value and Erotic Pleasure This Book Will Give You and Your Lover

1.1 The What and the How ~

The pleasure promise

This book demonstrates how to seduce a woman's body and mind so that you can introduce her to anal play with a detailed step-by-step method that gradually and painlessly enables couples to enjoy the pleasures of anal sexuality. The book will explain the strategies and reasons why the techniques work better than other books available in the marketplace. You will learn how to implement the 7 Nights to Ecstasy System, the SEPOR Method, with 76 illustrations, and 20 product recommendations, which are what makes this book the best guide on how to take it slow so she experiences painless pleasure. There are several books on the market for general anal sex, and they all give some minor tips that advise couples to take it "slow." What exactly defines "slow" is ambiguous and comes without a detailed explanation. Lack of detailed information is especially a hindrance when talking about anal sex because, if you mess up once, you probably won't get another try. That is the story of many women who tried it once but won't do it again because their partners went too fast, and it hurt! This book solves that problem! You will discover exactly how to take it slow in a way that will arouse and pleasure her at every step of the way. She will yearn for more and end up loving anal sex! This book will address:

- Psychological and physical concerns
- Communication
- Building trust
- Strategy explanations – how to give her exciting pleasure, one small step at a time
- Preparation for seducing her mind, body, soul, and all her senses
- The best toys to use and where to buy them
- The best lube and lube comparisons
- Hygiene and techniques to feel, smell, taste, and be deliciously clean
- The 7 Nights to Ecstasy System and SEPOR Method of arousing her anal orgasms
- Advanced techniques – thrilling cunnilingus, analingus, anal play techniques and positions to create hot erotic experiences, even for experienced lovers

1.2 For Whom ~
Erotic delight for women and couples

I wrote this book to enhance a woman's sexual realm of experience, so more women can enjoy incredible sexual pleasure, amazing orgasms, and deep intimacy, as well as express their erotic souls through the exploration and enjoyment of anal play. All the above applies to the joy couples will experience from anal sexuality. Many people are curious, many women have had bad experiences because guys typically move too quickly, some have psychological barriers, and some have health concerns. In this book, I will address all these issues and provide a solution for the fear many women have—that it is going to hurt! When a woman is introduced properly to anal sexuality, every step of the way will be pleasurable and exciting. If the process I provide in this book is performed with caring sensuality and erotic passion, women will not go through pain but will experience very intimate and erotic pleasure.

Therefore, this book is dedicated to the beauty of women and to expanding their sexuality to another level of ecstasy. For men, you are going to enjoy every step of the way, too! The process will be extremely enjoyable, and both of you are going to experience an immense amount of sexual fun. Guys, once you have taken the time to read the book thoroughly, and your woman is loving anal sex, cumming from it, and wanting more, you will be even happier in your sex life because you will more than double the number of positions and activities to enjoy.

For couples, anal play opens so much more sexual variety. It will spice up your love life and even provide more intimacy. If you are introducing anal sexuality to a relationship, it will bring you closer if it is done right. If you do it wrong, then it might bring the opposite, so make sure you read this book closely. Some guys repeatedly ask for anal sex, and girls resent them for doing so; this book will solve that. Once a woman starts experiencing the simultaneous stimulation of multiple erogenous zones, she will be aroused into having explosive full-body orgasms from anal sex with you!

1.3 Why ~
The unmet need to provide a detailed and illustrated, step-by-step system to painless anal pleasure

There are other books on the subject; but, after studying them, I realized not one had a detailed and illustrated, step-by-step process to make it pleasurable and painless for women. Other books have great information on the history of anal sex, reasons why people do it, why they do not engage in anal play, the anatomy of the anus, physiology of the body, different types of anal acts, different toys, health, hygiene, principles of anal sex, and mostly illustrations of anatomy. That is important information, and several are good books, but I felt they were missing the solution to one of the biggest problems of engaging in anal sexuality: How do you arouse your woman to try it? What are the best ways to overcome negative perceptions? How can you make it a pleasurable, painless process that she loves because of the great orgasms she will experience? I bought all the books I could find on anal sexuality.

Here are the books I found:

1. *The Ultimate Guide to Anal Sex for Women* – Tristan Taormino

2. *The Anal Sex Position Guide* – Tristan Taormino

3. *Anal Pleasure and Health – A guide for Men and Women* – Jack Morin Ph.D.

4. *Anal Sex for Couples – A Guaranteed Guide to Painless Pleasure* – Bill Strong with Lori Gammon

5. *Dare...to Have Anal Sex* – Coralie Trinh Thi

6. *How to Get Her to Watch Porn, Have Anal Sex, and Call Her Best Friend for a Threesome* – Sindy Powers and Cindy Powers

7. *Nina Hartley's Guide to Total Sex* – Nina Hartley

Why would I provide the books of my competitors? I would love for readers to compare these books to this one. I presented the books to a variety of female friends, and the consensus was the same. None of the books made the women feel that having their men read them would thoroughly prepare the men to build trust and introduce pleasurable, pain-free, anal sexuality into their love lives. Without that security, you cannot achieve the results you desire. Women need to feel secure that a man knows how to give them ecstatic anal pleasure without them fearing pain and feeling anxiety. The other books did not offer enough illustrations nor a sufficiently detailed, step-by-step method for them to feel secure in him knowing how to make sure it did not hurt.

The books did not present their chapters, content, and images in a manner that would arouse a woman into wanting to try anal play. The books provided tips and "how to" suggestions, but did not provide visual stimulation and a step-by-step system that the women felt excited to engage in. All the books stated "take it slow" but did not do a thorough job of defining what "taking it slow" means, so that women could trust the guy had all the knowledge he needed to make it pleasurable and painless. It is like telling someone to go slow on the freeway without providing a speed limit. In this book you will learn the speed that makes the process smooth.

The goals of this book are getting women to gradually enjoy anal sexuality in a pleasurable manner, to entice and arouse women into wanting to enjoy more... and more. The books mentioned above are good for overall anal knowledge, but not for comfortably introducing a woman to anal sex, especially if she has an interest, but is hesitant or scared. I felt the books also did not provide enough detail on the intro phase. This book's contents are designed with the sole purpose of arousing women and with the intent that they will want their partner to implement the techniques the book teaches. Test it by going to a bookstore with a female friend who hasn't done anal and one who has. Review the books listed above, and compare them to this book. You will clearly see which method she would prefer you implement. I was encouraged to write this book by girlfriends in my life who stated that I should put my technique down on paper. They were confident that many more women would be happy because of it, and these women would not have to go through bad experiences when trying anal sexuality. My girlfriends stated it would help many couples enjoy the delights of anal sexuality, and women would enjoy a new way of having incredible orgasms.

I wrote this book to focus on the introduction phase of anal sexuality, which tends to be the most challenging part of enjoying anal sex. What this book is not is an overall guide on anal sex. I did not want to replicate good work already out there. In this book I recommend other good books to read on different topics, such as in-depth research on the history of anal sexuality, social views, and extreme anal activities, such as "fisting," to name a few topics. You will not find this kind of information in this book, so I provide you resources on where to find the information. You will find that this book is the best anal sexuality introduction guide on the market that you can use to pleasure your woman so she can love anal sexuality for the joy and intimacy it will give both of you.

1.4. The Solution and Benefits ~
All the HOT rewards you will experience

The solution is not about trying to convince a woman to do anal by talking her into trying it. The solution is to seduce and pleasure the body and mind simultaneously to provide consistent and amazing pleasure, to take her from "NO" or "maybe" to "OMG that feels incredible!!!" The process involves pleasurable patience that is specifically defined. The benefits of pleasurable patience are as follows:

1. Provide a lot of erotic fun for both partners.

2. Give women the most incredible orgasms of their lives from anal sexuality.

3. Enable men to pleasurably teach women how to enjoy anal sexuality.

4. More than doubling your sexual fun when you expand into anal sexuality. Now you can do most all the activities anally as well. In addition there are activities involving pleasure to the pussy and the ass simultaneously that will provide you with new pleasures.

5. Reach a very deep level of intimacy and passion with anal sex.

6. Significantly increase the sense of novelty and wildness in your love life and sex life.

7. Build better trust and communication in your sex life.

1.5 The Difference ~
The pleasurable difference a couple will feel using the techniques in this book and EroticFlow.com

Men, you will give her the patience she needs to feel comfortable, and trust in your ability to take it slow, making the process pleasurable. You will not feel like you are missing out, or that it is not going fast enough. You will feel that the process is HOT; you will enjoy what you experience; and you will both look forward to the next step. My philosophy, strategy, and implementation of the process are deliciously different. She will be very happy that you read this book and implemented the methods within it. I provided are many visuals to illustrate exactly what to do. The book *Anal Sex for Couples* does not have one single image. Its author states, "Like you, I've done my exploring in the dark where black and white drawings are useless. I learned human anatomy by Braille and that is how I teach." I almost did not want to read on, the only reason I did was because I was doing competitive research. The content on introducing a woman to anal was lacking, too. I did my exploring with the lights on because my partners were sexy, hot, and beautiful!

Therefore, the differences between my book and the others are as follows:

1. **A different strategy that arouses the body to seduce the mind** by trying small steps that lead to anal pleasure. You are not going to try to talk her into trying it in one night; small pleasures will span seven nights.

2. A detailed, step-by-step system that defines "taking it slow," which I call "**The 7 Nights to Ecstasy System.**"

3. A method for providing her with lots of pleasure that is associated with anal stimulation every step of the way. This method is called "**The SEPOR Method.**"

4. **76 Illustrations** that: a) communicate what to do and how; b) deliver the content in a sensual and artistic fashion; and c) are designed to progressively arouse the visual senses of the female reader and inspire her desire to try anal play and the 7 Nights to Ecstasy System.

5. My recommendations on **the best anal toys and lubes** (with a lube comparison chart and 20 product images) for the intro phase. You'll learn **where to buy them at a discount.**

6. **Fun hygiene strategies** that will make preparation a hot experience too. As well as a customized system for your woman's experience.

7. **Unique anal play and advanced positions** with illustrations and more detail on how to do them than other resources.

8. The combination of this step-by-step system, with this number of instructional illustrations, arousal techniques, and gem entry techniques are not found in any other book, DVD, online video, blog, or web articles. Erotic explanations of the system and techniques.

9. **The Erotic Flow Members website,** where you'll have access to **Anal Orgasm Video** links, so the woman who is exploring anal pleasure can see other women genuinely enjoying and having orgasms from anal sex.

10. **The Erotic Flow shop** where you can buy the **DVD VERSION of THIS BOOK,** the **NEW EF TOY,** erotic music, erotic kits, and sexy clothing. **Erotic Flow education webinars and private consulting are also available.**

Chapter Summary

Chapter One ~ Introduction ~
The Unique Value and Erotic Pleasures
This Book Will Give You and Your Lover

1.1 The What and the How ~
The pleasure promise and how will this book deliver it

The 7 Nights to Ecstasy System and the SEPOR Method give a defined strategy on how to take it slow with your woman so the process of anal sexuality is pleasurable for her from beginning to end.

Communication, building trust, and proper preparation are **important**.

1.2 For Whom ~
Erotic delight for women and couples

For women who are interested or whose man is interested in having and enjoying anal sexuality; for men who are interested or have a woman who wants them to become knowledgeable about how to introduce her to anal sexuality; and for couples who want to expand their realms of passionate and erotic pleasure.

1.3 Why ~
The unmet need to provide a detailed, step-by-step system to painless anal pleasure

The other books on the market do not provide a step-by-step guide on how to take it slow; therefore, this book was developed. If you go to fast, you will hurt your woman, and she will not trust you. Most likely, she will not want to try again or will be irritated by your requests.

1.4 *The Solution and Benefits* ~

All the HOT rewards you will experience

The SEPOR Method and the 7 Nights to Ecstasy System. Your woman will experience amazing orgasms from anal play and anal sexuality. You will give her new delights of pleasure all throughout the process. You and your woman will attain new heights of intimacy and passion.

1.5 *The Difference* ~

The pleasurable difference in the techniques this book and EroticFlow.com deliver

a. A different strategy that arouses the body to seduce the mind.

b. 76 illustrations to effectively communicate what to do and how to do it.

c. The best anal toys, my favorite lubes, and where to buy them with discounts.

d. Fun preparation and customized system

e. Unique anal play activities, advanced techniques, and erotic dialogue. Erotic Dialogue explanation in Resources section.

f. The FIRST MULTIMEDIA BOOK experience at EroticFlow.com.

g. EroticFlow.com website with video chapter summaries and printable chapter summaries.

Visit the website for the latest information on erotic sexuality. Coming soon: Videos, Music, Blog, Fashion, Toys, Social Networking, Events, and More!!!

Chapter Two
Arouse Her Mind, Body, and Soul

~≈≈~

The Path to Flowing Together with the SEPOR Method and 7 Nights to Ecstasy

2.1 Satisfy Her Soul ~
So you can discover new pleasures with trust

So, let's get started! I originally was going to call the book "Gem Pleasure" because throughout the book I refer to a woman's anal ring and the inside as her "gem." "Gem" is the term I thought of because it is a beautiful and precious part of her body that can give her lots of sexual satisfaction. Along with the genital areas, the gem is connected to and interwoven with millions of delicately sensitive nerve endings, which can yield incredibly pleasurable sensations. To inspire her to be open to enjoying ecstasy there, you are going to have to fall in love with pleasuring her everywhere—her mind, body, and soul. When you are pleasuring her, you get lost in that moment; there is nothing else that exists, and every ounce of your energy is there. It feels like you are coming to orgasm from giving her pleasure and making her feel incredible. She will notice your passion.

So, let's stimulate her mind and soul, and talk about intimacy. Although this is not a book on relationships, communication and intimacy are important when venturing into anal sexuality. Since anal sex is a very intimate experience, you and your partner should have good communication and a playful attitude towards trying new things in the bedroom. Make sure you know what makes her feel most cared for or loved by you. Find out her "must have" to feel cared for: Is it what you do for her and how you do those things? Is it the things you say and how you say them? Or is it the kinesthetic feeling she has when you hold each other? Do all three but make sure you deliver well on her "must have."

Find out how she likes to express caring/love. Tell her your "must have" for receiving caring/love and how you like to express it. To have her be open to sexual exploration, you first need to put in the effort to make sure she feels appreciated, beautiful, cared for, sexy, and important. She needs to feel comfortable with you and feel that she can trust you to listen to her if she says to slow down or stop due to discomfort from going too fast, and that you will gladly listen. **Building trust is crucial**—just put yourself in her shoes. You need to let her know that it does not matter how long it takes because you are there to give her pleasure and enjoy each other's passion. Let her know that even if it takes weeks or months for her, it does not matter because you are there to enjoy the sensual and erotic experiences of the journey. The 7 Nights to Ecstasy System provides a minimum number of nights to make it happen, but depending on your size and your woman, you might need to add more nights. That is okay! You will get there and be happy that you enjoyed the journey.

If you get impatient, you will go too fast and hurt her, and typically, that will be the end of the ride because it will be hard to trust you again. So, in terms of her mind, I am not promoting that you try to persuade her psychologically to want to try it. Instead, psychologically, you need to do things, say things, and hold her in ways that make her feel beautiful, sexy, and appreciated. There are many books on relationships, communication, and sexuality. Read them, and become a master at making her feel incredible, both physically and mentally. She will be much more receptive to sexual exploration and adventure when you have more knowledge on the variety of subjects you need in order to make sure that all her emotional bases are covered. These steps will also help you explore with confidence. This experience is about flowing together in the moment, and having her erotic energy and passion becoming one with yours. The erotic seduction of a woman's mind, body, and soul is the art and passion of my soul. If you make it yours, your woman will be very happy and you'll be rewarded. Become a master of kissing her in a variety of ways that really turn her on. Kissing connects people deeply. Make it your art to kiss her and her entire body with all your soul. Use your lips, tongue, and kisses to tease and excite her sensuality. Entice the erotic side of her soul to come out and play. Take the time to kiss her deliciously and connect with her throughout the entire journey of arousing her anal ecstasy.

2.2 Seduce Her Body ~

So her mind eagerly wants more ~ The SEPOR Method

Here is an overview of a typical situation: A woman usually does not want to try anal because of some reason or another. Most typically, she does not know the incredible pleasure she can receive from it, or she thinks the process of getting there will hurt. Many women also factor in religion and hygiene reasons as well. Most of these reasons can be overcome, not by trying to talk her into it, but by slowly showing her body how good it can feel. By gradually and strategically demonstrating to her body the pleasure it can feel from light anal play, she will slowly be open to more and more.

The SEPOR Method is about starting with small steps, showing her pleasure, and rewarding her with explosive orgasms at every step. **The SEPOR Method is as follows:**

S - Stimulate   Stimulate her so as to arouse her senses, body, erogenous zones, and her personal zones of pleasure. Sensually and passionately get her in the mood.

E - Excite   Excite her body with a new experience of arousal. The first time it will be just massaging the outer gem. The second time you will be licking the outer gem. Each time you bring a small but exciting new experience of exploration.

P - Pleasure   Spend time pleasuring her with the new experience. Indulge in enjoying the moment. Flow together in the moment with every caress and every lick. Just enjoy doing the act for a time without a goal.

O - Orgasm   After thoroughly enjoying the new experience, add stimulation that you know will bring her to orgasm. Continue to perform the new experience while you make her orgasm with what you know she loves, so she associates lots of pleasure with the new experience.

R - Reaffirm   Talk to her about the experience. Find out what she liked most, if there were things she did not like, or things you might not have done that she would have liked.

Every night has something new, so talk to her about every new experience. Ask about speed, places that felt good or not, angling of your cock, fingers, and toys. Communicate in the moment to adjust on the fly and afterwards. You don't want to devote a lot of time to doing something she did not like, only to find out afterwards. Look at her facial expressions and body reactions for signs on how to adjust. Communicate how much you enjoy it and how much it turns you on. Ask her questions in a sexy way.

The SEPOR Method makes every step of the process an incredibly pleasurable experience. The O in the SEPOR Method stands for orgasm. If you know what makes her orgasm, do that, but do not focus solely on the goal of getting her to orgasm. Indulge in the pleasuring of her, and let her feel that all your passion and energy is being sent to her in every lick, kiss, suck, and caress. When you both get lost in the moment without a goal, you will thoroughly enjoy the amazing pleasure you both are experiencing. She can feel your heart, soul, and how turned on you are from experiencing that passion together, and that is when she will tend to orgasm.

The general advice out there is to go slowly, but I will provide a sense of measurement by limiting what and how you should do things. You will have a guideline for how much to do for a given night and how much time you should (down to the minutes and seconds) spend on some techniques. Some women will be able to go faster, and you may have a desire to do so. Though you might have this situation, stick to the 7 Nights to Ecstasy System, as it will provide a baseline and it will be fun to go through. If she wants you to go faster because she has done an activity before, then go to the next night's activities, and see how she feels. Remember, if you go too fast, and you do too much, she will have a bad experience, and that will probably end the fun. Make it an exciting game of body exploration for the woman you are passionate about.

2.3 Communication ~

Arousing her sexuality to new exciting heights: The 7 Nights to Ecstasy System

Other books on anal begin by right away going through the process; they make the mistake of assuming the woman is already willing to try it. Many times, however, if a woman has never done it, she might be hesitant. This book is going to make the hesitant woman feel more comfortable about exploring the anal pleasure process. As stated before, the method used in this book starts with arousing her body and then seeking feedback from her mind. Initially, you are going to take the time to arouse her body fully. That means all of her other erogenous zones: her lips, cheeks, neck, ears, shoulders, back, small of back, stomach, pelvic bones (lower stomach towards her sides), arms, hands, fingers, thighs, calves, feet, toes, breasts, pussy, and clitoris. Eventually it will be time for dessert—her gem.

Make sure that during and after you arouse her you get feedback on how she likes the things you've done. Does she like biting? How deep, how wide, where, and what kind of kisses does she like? What type of play does she like? Soft and sensual, more intense and rough, or all of the above in the right sequence? So, once you get down to licking her pussy, you want to become a Jedi Master at cunnilingus of her entire body, to bring her to love the Freak Side of the Force (lol). Become a master of erotic talk before, during, and after sensual and erotic experiences. Let her know how hot she is, how much she turns you on, how much you enjoy her body, how sexy she moves, how delicious she tastes, how much you enjoy the way she sounds, how good she feels (every part), and let her know what things turn you on.

Find out what language turns both of you on, and use it throughout. You can even turn each other on with emails or texts to make the nights more exciting until you are with each other again. Once you get further into the process, you should talk about what terms and statements turn you on, so you can use the language that will have the most powerful effect. These statements will get more provocative and hotter as you progress through the system, so at least do so by Night 3, then again for Night 5, and again at Night 7. Continue the dialogue in case you think of new things you want to hear and/or to discover new things she wants to hear. Find out how you want them said, too. The "how" matters as much as the "what."

2.4 The 7 Nights to Ecstasy System ~
The solution

Night 1 Excite and pleasure her by only massaging the outer gem with your finger while licking her clitoris and her pussy. Implement the SEPOR Method.

Night 2 Pleasure her by licking her outer gem, while playing with her clitoris and pussy. Lick her pussy and gem while using your fingers to provide simultaneous pleasure. Start with Night 1 techniques. Implement the SEPOR Method.

Night 3 Pleasure her by licking her clitoris and pussy, massaging her G-Spot, inserting a finger into her gem. Pinky finger first, then your middle finger. Start with Night 1 and 2 techniques. Use the SEPOR Method throughout.

Night 4 Pleasure her with a beginner anal vibrating toy and two fingers (not at same time) while licking her clitoris, and massaging her G-Spot. Implement techniques from Nights 1, 2, 3, and the SEPOR Method. Try to move on to Night 5 within five nights to maintain conditioning.

Night 5 Pleasure her with a gradually bigger girth toy and three fingers (not at same time) while licking her clitoris and massaging her G-Spot. Implement techniques from Nights 1, 2, 3, and 4, plus the SEPOR Method. Depending on his size, this night might need to be repeated with another, bigger toy closer to the girth of his size. Night 6 should occur within five nights to maintain progress.

Night 6 Warm her up with techniques from Nights 1 through 5, then put a toy on her clitoris, use entering techniques, and insert yourself very slowly and sensually with simultaneous stimulation to her outer gem, pussy, and nipples. SEPOR. Missionary and slower sensual movements only. Night 7 should occur within five nights.

Night 7 Warm her up with techniques from Nights 1 through 6. Move on to deeper, faster movements and different positions; while having a toy on her clitoris, stimulate her pussy, G-Spot, and other erogenous zones. Delight her with the Chapter 5 anal play techniques, SEPOR, and sex that will give her explosive orgasms.

The key is to make every new small step during each night an experience that pleasures her deeply, so each night brings her to orgasm while stimulating her gem and leaves her yearning for more next time. Nights 1, 2, and 3 can be done consecutively, though it would be good to take at least a one-night break between each Nights 3 and 4. You can take a longer break in between Nights 4-7, but I recommend no more than four to five nights, because if you wait too long, you might lose some of the progress you've made.

Communication about the process and how it feels during all nights is important. As you progress, see what turns her on and how she likes things. Get specifics when engaging in the process on slower, faster, harder, softer, or changing positions, etc. In order to introduce anal play, one very important factor is trust. Trust is built over time and by consistently delivering on your word. Even though you two might trust each other in other aspects of your relationship, it is good to build her trust in you, your skills, and your intentions in this aspect—don't just assume she will trust you. An important factor of the 7 Nights to Ecstasy System is that you are going to build trust over time by consistently delivering on your word, that you are going to go slow, you are going to stop if something is uncomfortable, and you are going to listen to her feelings and sensations so you can adjust accordingly. As the nights progress, her trust will build; she will relax and enjoy because you have delivered on your word every time. It is all about the exploration of erotic ecstasy and how you build her trust in you, throughout this journey of pleasure.

Another aspect of communication is the deep intimacy you will experience with your partner during anal sex. Other books and DVDs usually advise or show a woman starting anal play in a bent-over-on-all-fours position. This position is great once she has already started enjoying anal fondling and licking, but if she has never done any anal play, it is better that she start on her back. In the beginning, you want to start with a position that is more intimate and provides easy communication. By starting with her on her back and doing everything you would do in the initiation of sensual experience in missionary position, you will build intimacy. You are about to engage in an act that can be viewed as one of the most intimate in the sexual realm. It has definitely provided a deep sense of connection and erotic intimacy for thousands of lovers. It is important for you to see her facial expressions and gauge her comfort. You want this view, since you are going to pleasure her and then seek feedback with communication to make sure she is enjoying every step of the journey.

2.5 Assess How She Feels About Anal Play ~
Design the process for her & the 3-Night Delight System

Tell her that you want to satisfy all of her sexual desires and fantasies. It is your pleasure to give her pleasure and to excite all of her senses. Is there something she would like to experience, because you would enjoy making that fantasy come to life? Then ask her what kind of things she has tried or has found she likes. Ask about sex in different locations, positions, toys, hair pulling, spanking, biting, a hand or two sensually holding her neck, and anal play. You should ask about a variety of sensual activities before the anal play question. After each question, if she says she has not tried something, ask her if she has ever been curious or interested in trying that activity. Use the above system to cover a variety of sex activities, so it flows naturally when you get to the anal play question.

If she says that she has never tried anal sex and was never interested, then start from the beginning of the 7 Nights to Ecstasy System, implementing all your previous communication and the actions needed to make her feel cared for, appreciated, beautiful, and very sexy. Spend quality time to arouse her, then implement Nights 1 through 4. Do not implement if you don't have enough time to make it really good for her. Once you get through the first several nights of the system, you will know her level of interest because you have taken small steps of pleasure towards her enjoyment of anal play. If she is liking the experience, then continue. If you are going too fast, then repeat the beginning nights. It might take longer—that is okay. Your objective is not to get to the end quickly. You need to enjoy pleasuring her, and she truly needs to feel that from you.

When she trusts that you have her best interest at heart, you will be able to expand each other's realm of experience.

If she states that she never tried it but is interested, start from the beginning. After Night 2, show her the book. It is designed for showing to a woman, and she will see that you have spent the time to make sure that she has a pleasurable experience throughout. If she states that she has tried anal play before, then get an honest assessment about the most she has done and how long it has been. Read the activities in the 7 Nights to Ecstasy System to know what to ask. For example, do you enjoy having your gem licked? Or, how about a finger in your gem while someone licks your clitoris? If she has done any anal play before but not in the last six months, then start from the beginning. It is safer to start at the beginning of my method and work your way back up, even if she has previous experience, to ensure her experience with you will always be pleasurable.

If she has done anal play before and it was within six months, then find out what she has experienced. You should implement all the pleasuring techniques from the 7 Nights system in a single session until you reach what she has done before. Spend time making her feel incredible with what she is already comfortable with and continue from that point forward using the system as instructed. Another option is covered next.

The 7 Nights to Ecstasy system, option 1, is for women who are new to anal play or are scared of anal sex for one reason or another. Option 2, the **3-Night Delight System,** is for more advanced couples that have experience with anal play. Assess her experience to see if this is a better solution for you.

The **3-Night Delight System** is as follows:

Night 1 Excite and pleasure with the activities of the Nights 1, 2, and 3 of the 7 Nights System. Implement the SEPOR Method.

Night 2 Start with by pleasuring her with the activities of massaging her gem, licking it, and playing with your fingers. Then use the techniques from Nights 4 and 5 of the 7 Nights System. Use the dilation system to a girth close to your girth. Remember simultaneous pleasure, Pleasure Twists (covered later), and the SEPOR Method.

Night 3 Arouse and stimulate her gem with the pleasuring techniques from Nights 1 and 2 of the Delight System. Then, implement the techniques from Nights 6 and 7. Make sure you use the 5 Steps to Enter Her Gem (covered in Night 6). Since this will be the first time you are entering her gem with your cock be conscious of not going for too long. You don't want her to be sore. So do it for as long as it is feeling really good to her. Ask her to tell you if she experiences any discomfort. At first sign of any discomfort, pause and use the exit technique described in Night 6. Then focus on pleasuring her incredibly with her favorite stimulation techniques to bring her to orgasm.

If on Night 3 she still needs more time, let her know it is ok and it does not matter how long it takes, it is about the pleasure you two are experiencing. Remember, if you let go of any time pressures, she can then focus on enjoying the arousal techniques. Then, it is up to you to make her feel incredible in order to progress further. Option 3 is the **Custom System,** if options 1 or 2 do not seem to provide the best solution. If she has a lot of anal play experience, you can implement all the pleasuring techniques from the 7 Nights System in a single session until you reach what she has done before. Spend time making her feel incredible with what she has already done and continue from that point forward using the remaining night-by-night system from the 7 Nights. Account for her experience, her physiology, your girth, and building trust and arousal so she yearns for it. The Custom System can be two nights for a woman with a lot of anal play experience with thicker toys or with two or more male fingers past second knuckle. When in doubt add a day. Also, can be much more than 7 nights for couples who's specific situation needs more time. View the Chapter Summary for an important note on a 1 night attempt.

2.6 Night 1 ~
Beginning a new world of pleasure

After implementing my communication advice, you are now ready to begin Night 1. Have her lay on her back. Kiss, lick, and caress her lips, neck, shoulders, breasts, nipples, stomach, pelvic area, thighs, and all her erogenous zones. As you are kissing her, start lightly playing with her clitoris and her pussy with your fingers. Have her spread her legs wide, so you have access to her gem. Here, you are going to move from kissing her lips to her breasts and her stomach while simultaneously caressing her clitoris and pussy lips lightly [**See Image 2.1**].

You want to spend time getting her really wet in this manner while slowly applying more passion to your caress of her pussy. Slowly dip the tip of your finger in her pussy to let more wetness out. As your finger starts to get wetter, go in a little deeper and put slight pressure downward to massage the bottom of her pussy, an arousal area called the perineal sponge. The downward massage will

2.1

stimulate her and allow more wetness to come out from her pussy, so you can guide it down to her tang (the area in between her pussy and gem). Spread the wetness around her tang with your finger while caressing her clitoris with your thumb. See how she reacts to you going up and down from her pussy to her tang [See Image 2.2]. Most women will be okay with this. Tell her in hot sexual manner during the foreplay, that you want to massage around and over her gem and that you have no intention of inserting your fingers in her gem. You just want to caress her entire whole body to see how she likes it. Let your finger take longer strokes up and down, making sure your thumb continues to caress her clitoris and pussy at the same time you are kissing her lips and breasts. Bring her wetness to the areas right around her gem. Lightly caress your middle finger

2.2

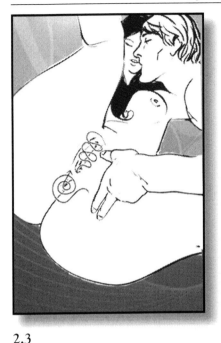

2.3

over her gem and kiss her passionately; come back up to circle her pussy. You don't want to focus too much on her gem in the beginning. Alternate the pleasure between where she is comfortable and the new area of exploration. This method does not involve any surprise moves. Then go back down and start to caress her in circular motions around her gem.

Now you are just going to stimulate the outside of the gem and around the center of her gem, but you are not going to try to penetrate the gem at this time. You just want her to enjoy the stimulation of the area while she is also lost in your kisses and stimulation of other areas. Get her gem really wet with her juices, and as you continue to play with her clitoris, put some of your thumb in her pussy as your fingers play with her gem [**See Image 2.3**]. You can put a little more sensual pressure on the gem, but do not try to go in. Do this for a while, so she can get used to the stimulation of her clitoris, pussy lips, tang, and gem.

Another stimulation technique is called the **Finger Roll**. Lubricate her clitoris and gem generously, position your hand like in the previous image **2.2** with your thumb on her clitoris, and massage her clitoris while placing your pinky at the bottom of her gem. Then, slide your pinky up across her gem, follow it with your ring finger, middle finger, and first finger. Roll all fingers slowly and sensually while applying a little pressure. Speed up a little and change the direction of the roll. Do all this while you are playing with her clitoris with your thumb. Your other hand can be playing with her nipples while you suck her nipples as well.

The next stimulation technique is the **Palm & Gem Pleasure**. Again, lubricate her clitoral area generously so that the lubrication across her clitoris extends to the size of your palm. You are going to place the top of your palm on her clitoris, and then your first finger is going to sensuously massage her gem and all around it. Your middle finger can massage her tang, and your ring finger can go inside of her pussy to massage her G-Spot. Massage her clitoris with your palm by going in a circular motion, up and down, and side to side, while using your first finger to play with her gem. Your middle and ring finger play inside and outside her pussy [See Image 2.4].

Depending on your woman's previous sexual experience and comfort level

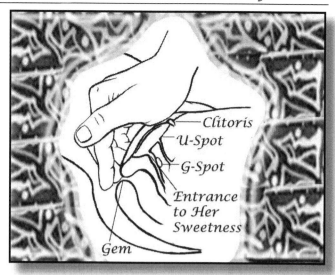

2.4

with this type of gem play up to this point, you can move on to more foreplay and pleasuring her in the same way as during regular sex. **IMPORTANT:** Lick her clitoris while you sensually massage around and over her gem using the finger play techniques explained for this night. Use all parts of your hand, both front and back of fingers, to provide variety. While having sex sensually massage around the gem area and lightly on her gem and tang with your fingers. Imagine sending warm energy to your fingers while you massage her gem area. Use the techniques above, Night 2 clitoral licking with gem massaging, and a variety of positions, like the **E3 and V-Spot Massage** activities in Chapter 5, but DO NOT go inside her gem with your fingers. Just stimulate the outside for now. If she has not had this type of anal play before, then let this be it for Night 1. Remember to give her a great orgasm, the way you know how. Include the gem play described above, so she associates lots of pleasure to gem play, as she orgasms. If she has done this before and is very comfortable with it, then you can move on to Night 2.

2.7 Night 2 ~

Feel the warmth of my passion

If she enjoyed Night 1—and most women will— continue to the next stage of pleasure. You are going to use erotic cunnilingus to take her to the next stage. Take a shower together. Then place her on her back. On her back, she will feel a deeper sense of connection, intimacy, and comfort than in doggy

Kiss
Lick
Bite
Kiss
Lick
Suck
Bite
Lick
Kiss
Suck
Sensuous bite
Deep sensuous bite
Lick

Sensually glaze your tongue across her lips under her clitoris but not on it yet. You are deliciously teasing her senses at this point.

2.5

style position. You can also gauge her looks and reactions as you start engaging in stimulating her gem.

After doing all the foreplay of Night 1, with her legs in the air, start the cunnilingus from her feet or ankles and work your way up to her calves in circular motions. Go on to her thighs, and take deep sensuous bites of her inner thigh as you get closer to her sweetness, her sweet pussy. As you get to her pussy, slow down. Lick on the outside of her pussy and all around the area between her lips and legs. Lick her slowly and very passionately. Take deep, soft, sensuous bites into that area [See Image 2.5]. (It is best to have your woman shave this area very well, so she can fully feel the warmth and wetness of your tongue.)

Then, start near her leg and begin to glaze her pussy with the wetness of your tongue. Move across her pussy very lightly, so she can feel the warmth of your breath and lightly feel the warm wetness of your tongue as you go across to the other side. Take the same sensuous, soft, deep bites on the other side and come back to glaze across again. This time let more of your tongue touch her.

Then, lick her up and down lightly. You can pass over several more times, each time pleasuring her more and more. Let yourself flow in the moment by letting all your passion come across and directing all your energy to your mouth, lips, and tongue. Treat her wetness like it is your favorite dessert in the world. Let the passion drip from your tongue onto her clitoris and lips.

As you continue to lick her for a while, start taking longer strokes down towards her gem. First, just go down to her tang, and see how she reacts. Most likely, she will react well if you have taken the time to passionately arouse her. Let her enjoy the play on her tang for a bit.

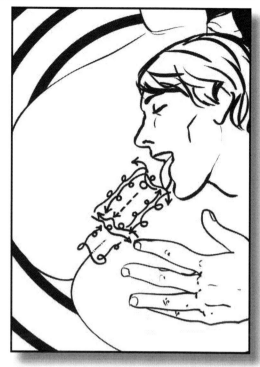

2.6

Start massaging her clitoris lightly with your fingers. Get her to enjoy the simultaneous stimulation of you playing with her tang and licking her clitoris. Move your tongue downward and head to the area around her gem, but not the gem yet [**See Image 2.6**]. Stay there for several seconds and come back up to lick her pussy again, while still playing with her clitoris. With hot sexual talk, let her know you want to caress her gem area with your tongue and you have no intention of inserting your fingers, just pleasuring her gem area with your tongue, to see how she likes that. As you go back up this time, turn your head to the side, and from the bottom put both of her lips inside your lips and your tongue in between her lips. Suck upwards as the warmth of your wet tongue licks sensually and stimulates her in between her lips to her clitoris. Sensually suck, lick, and kiss her clitoris at the top. Do all of the above while sensuously massaging her gem with your fingers.

Each time you go back down to her gem area, play softly and sensuously with your tongue in order to let her wetness and the wetness of your tongue start glazing the area around her gem and on the gem itself. Gauge her pleasure and comfort level the closer you get. Her gem has many nerve

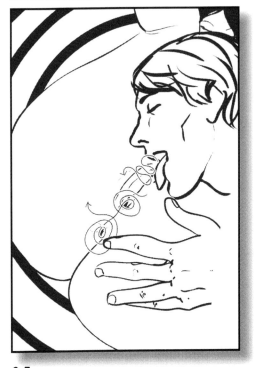

2.7

2.8

endings that make stimulation of this area very pleasurable and very noticeable. Circle your fingers around her gem.

Start circling your tongue closer to her gem. Go back up to lick and indulge in her pussy, and then go back down. You are still stimulating and caressing her clitoris as you lightly glaze her gem with your tongue [**See Image 2.7**]. Lightly let out the warmth of your breath as you pass right over her gem while your lips are lightly circling it. The warm wetness of your tongue is going to feel good to her, and she is going to want you to lick more. Lick the fingers on your free hand, then stimulate her nipples with your wet fingers.

You want to provide simultaneous stimulation, so she can associate a lot of pleasure with the experience, so she does not feel like you are only focusing on her gem. Now, you are pleasuring multiple erogenous zones: fingers on nipples and clitoris and tongue on gem.

Lick around her anal ring softly, sensuously. Let her feel not only the stimulation of your tongue, but also the stimulation of all your energy and passion being directed towards her. If she continues to let you lick her, go back up to the pussy and kiss it softly, then more passionately, as though you were kissing her on the mouth. Just as though you were making out with her sensuously, pack as much emotion into the kiss as you can. The energy of the kiss should feel as though it is coming from the bottom of your heart and traveling up to your lips. She will feel the difference between you licking her to achieve an end goal and licking because you are engulfed in the moment, enjoying every lick. Write with your tongue in cursive on her clitoris, her pussy, her tang, and around her gem. Write how gorgeous she is, write hot sex talk, and tell her out loud what you are writing. Gather as much of her juices as possible on your lips and tongue. Use your

2.9

lips, tongue, and breath to kiss, suck, and write on her sweetness with all your passion **[See Image 2.8]**.

Start slowly, but apply a little more pressure and passion on the gem than previously, but not too hard. She still has to feel the softness of your tongue on and slightly in her gem. Let the wetness of your tongue drip a little onto her gem, and lick it a little deeper. All this time, you have been simultaneously stimulating her clitoris and her nipples. If she has let you do this, then she is game for more pleasuring with your tongue, and you can bring the hand on her nipples down to her pussy and clitoris. Use the middle finger of your left hand to play around her pussy, and then slowly insert your middle finger into her pussy. Have her move her legs back as far as possible to expose her gem more, for you to indulge in it. If her legs don't move back very far because of limited flexibility, then try putting a pillow under her ass to angle her gem higher; this will give you better access for licking it **[See Image 2.9]**.

Circle your tongue around her gem while you kiss and lick it. Go wider

2.10

around her ass cheeks, lightly bite and nibble on them. Go back to the center of and around her gem. You are simultaneously using your right-hand fingers to stimulate her clitoris while the left hand plays with her tongue and lips to gather wetness.

Come back down to caress the area around her gem and on her gem. Sensually play with her pussy and tang. Then, insert your first and/or middle fingers into her pussy. Simultaneously massage the inner areas of her pussy and perineal sponge, while you play with her clitoris with the thumb or fingers of your other hand. Circle your tongue in the middle of the gem. Begin to push lightly into the gem. Then lick around. Point your tongue, and try to enjoy a deeper licking of the center of her gem [**See Image 2.10**].

See how she reacts. If she is still in the moment, try to go deeper with your tongue. Remember to muster as much passion and emotion as possible-in your every lick, in your tongue, and in your lips, so she feels not only the physical pleasure but a connection to the strong, erotic energy and passion that you are sending her. Ask her to spread her ass cheeks with her hands for you, so you can go deeper with your tongue. Indulge in the play for as long as you would like her going down on you, and longer. Let this be Night 2. Remember, you are going to reward her with pleasure and orgasms at every step, so incorporate the gem play of the night while you give her a delicious orgasm. You want to leave her wanting more, fantasizing about how good it felt, yearning for more gem stimulation, and eager to continue play next time **[See Image 2.11]**. Patience is critical, but with this method the process will be incredibly pleasurable for both of you. Take the time to provide exhilarating pleasure and orgasms along the way. She will learn to LOVE gem play and sex.

Continue to have sex and play with her gem with your fingers and tongue throughout. As you are having sex, pull out, and lick her pussy and gem.

She is now accustomed to this stimulation and will welcome the pleasure in the different positions. Use a vibrator on her clitoris while you lick her gem as well.

Most women will enjoy this, just like most men would enjoy a woman sucking them and alternating between licking their cock down to the gem and back up, and licking while stroking them. This feels really good! More analingus play that can be used during Night 2 are techniques: **f. The Tongue Tingle, i. The Straddle and Flip, m. Eyes Wide Shut [image 5.22], p. Upside Down V-Lick, and x. Bottoms Up (your tongue can lick her Gem deeply, do not slide fingers deep inside yet).** These techniques are covered in chapter 5, "Erotic Anal Play – Delicious Stimulation for Both of You."

2.11

Night 3 will be explained after I cover some information you will need to know on hygiene and toys, because you are going to start playing inside her gem. I covered Nights 1 and 2 first because I want to give a woman reading this book a sense of the pleasure she will receive, so she will yearn for the next step of arousal and want to continue to learn and enjoy more.

Chapter Summary

〜〜

Chapter Two ~ Arouse Her Mind, Body, and Soul ~

The Path to Flowing Together with the SEPOR Method and the 7 Nights to Ecstasy System

2.1 Satisfy Her Soul ~
So you can discover new pleasures with trust

   a. The "gem" is the beautiful part of her that you will be playing with and entering.

   b. Build the intimacy, caring, flirtation, respect, passion, and trust outside the bedroom so things can flow inside the bedroom.

   c. Find out her "must haves" in terms of how she receives and expresses caring/love.

   d. Become a master of kissing her in a variety of ways that turn her on. Kiss her with all your soul to connect with her deeply. Make sure you take the time to kiss her deliciously and connect with her throughout the entire journey of arousing her anal ecstasy.

   e. Building trust is imperative!

2.2 Seduce Her Body ~
So her mind eagerly wants more ~ The SEPOR Method

   a. You are going to take only small steps to give her lots of pleasure, so she eagerly wants a little more. You will use this method throughout every night of the system you select.

b. The SEPOR Method

S = Stimulate - her senses and body the way she likes.

E = Excite - her body with a new experience of arousal, a new small step of pleasure.

P = Pleasure - spend time indulging in pleasuring her with the new experience combined with other things she enjoys.

O = Orgasm - after thoroughly pleasuring her in the new experience, combine it with what you know will give her a good orgasm, so she will associate the new experience with lots of pleasure.

R = Reaffirm - talk to her about the experience and find out what she liked, what you could have done differently, or if there was something she did not like. Let her know how much she turns you on and how beautiful she is, inside and out.

2.3 Communication ~
Arousing her sexuality to new exciting heights and the 7 Nights to Ecstasy System

a. Become a master of her intimate pleasures by communicating with her to find out exactly what drives her wild.

b. Let her know what you like and communicate to make her a master of your pleasures.

2.4 The 7 Nights to Ecstasy System ~
The solution

Night 1 Pleasure her by only massaging the outer gem with your finger while licking her clitoris and her pussy. SEPOR throughout.

Night 2 Pleasure her by licking her outer gem, while playing with her clitoris and pussy. Lick her pussy and gem while using your fingers to provide simultaneous pleasure. Start with Night 1 techniques.

Night 3   Pleasure her by licking her clitoris and pussy, massaging her G-Spot, and inserting a finger in her gem. Start with a pinky finger, then progress to your middle finger. Start with Night 1 and 2 techniques.

Night 4   Pleasure her with a beginner anal vibrating toy and two fingers (not at the same time) while licking her clitoris, and massaging her G-Spot. Circling methods were defined. Implement techniques 1, 2, and 3. Try to move on to Night 5 within five nights to maintain conditioning.

Night 5   Pleasure her with a gradually bigger girth toy or three fingers while licking her clitoris and massaging her G-Spot. Implement techniques 1, 2, 3, and 4, plus the SEPOR Method. Pleasure Twists and oooh OOOHs. Big-size guys might need this Night repeated with bigger toy closer to your girth. Try moving to Night 6 within five nights.

Night 6   Warm her up with techniques 1 through 5, then use the 5 Steps to Entering Her Gem. Try moving to Night 7 within five nights.

Night 7   Warm her up with techniques from Nights 1 through 6. Move on to deeper, faster movements and different positions while having a toy on her clitoris. Make sure you stimulate her pussy, G-Spot, U-Spot, and other erogenous zones. Continue to explore advanced play.

Nights 4 to 7 should have a one-night break in between.

Start with your woman on her back, so to see her facial expressions easily, communicate easily, and build the most intimacy possible for the journey into anal ecstasy. Designate a hand for anal massage and the other hand for pussy and clitoral massage.

2.5. *Assess How She Feels About Anal Play* ~
Design the process for her, 3-Night Delight System & Custom

Get an honest assessment of what she has done before in her sexual experimentation. Out of the experiences she has never tried, ask her if she has ever been interested in experiencing them, including anal play. If she says no to anal play, ask her why, so you know what specific concerns she has. That way you will know how to address this topic with her. The system is set up so it is a non-issue anyway, because you are only going to take small steps and only go as far as she likes. The key is that you are genuinely going to go only as far as she likes, but you are going to master pleasuring so thoroughly that she will gradually want more and more.

Find out her fantasies and new things she wants to try. Then make them happen for her and you. Use the **3-Night Delight System** if you are a couple with anal play experience. **IMPORTANT NOTE FOR A 1 NIGHT ATTEMPT:** The only time you should do it in 1 night, is in the following two situations. First, if she uses toys or other things that are really close to the size of your girth frequently in her Gem. Second, if she has had anal sex before, enjoyed it, and the guy was only a little bit smaller than you, then she knows she will have a good experience. If one of the above is the case, then follow the instructions of Night 6. Though, if either is not the case, it is better to add nights so you can build trust and pleasure.

2.6 *Night 1* ~
Beginning a new world of pleasure

a. Pleasure her by massaging only the outer gem with your finger while licking her clitoris and her pussy. Implement the SEPOR Method.

b. Lick, suck, and kiss all of her erogenous zones before you play around her outer gem, kissing her passionately all over her: neck, shoulders, arms, breasts, stomach, pelvic bone, sides, thighs, calves, feet, and toes. After that, start licking her sweetness.

c. **Tell her in hot sexual manner during the foreplay, that you want to massage around and over her gem and that you have** no intention of inserting your fingers in her gem, you just want to caress her entire whole body to see how she likes it. This is important, so she knows what to expect and she won't be scared of you trying to insert your fingers when you caress over her gem.

d. As you lick her clitoris, use your hands to massage thighs, lips, around her pussy, the area between her pussy and gem, her tang, then around her gem, then around the outer gem, but not inside. That is as far as you are going to go for anal play on Night 1. Bring her to orgasm while doing this.

2.7 *Night 2* ~

Feel the warmth of my passion

a. Start with Night 1 techniques and implement the SEPOR Method. As you sensually and passionately lick her pussy, move down to the area in between her pussy and gem. Lick and kiss there and come back up to her clitoris.

b. **With hot sexual talk, let her know you want to caress her gem area with your tongue and you have no intention of inserting your fingers,** just pleasuring her gem area with your tongue, to see how she likes that. Tell her you want to send all your passion to your tongue and lips; and that you want her to experience that around her gem. Remember, it's important that she knows what to expect, so she is not scared.

c. While you do that, massage the outer gem with your fingers, then go back down closer to her gem and come back up continuously to stimulate her outer gem. Keep doing this until you're sensually licking around her gem and playing with her clitoris at the same time.Continue to move up and down from clitoris to around the gem. Then sensually stay licking around her gem, and let the warmth of your tongue slightly go in the center of her gem while you play with her clitoris.

d. Thoroughly enjoy doing this for her. Then combine that with what you know will bring her to orgasm. Reaffirm – talk about what she liked, could have modified, or anything that she might not have enjoyed as much.

Enjoy erotic music playlists and EF's favorite YouTube videos on dating, relationships, sex, and more @:

YouTube.com/EroticFlow

Get Social @:

Facebook.com/EroticFlow

We love your likes!

Learn erotic facts and history @

Twitter.com/EroticFlow

Let's be friends and meet more friends @:

Facebook.com/DavidDeCitore

Chapter Three

Prepare for Pleasure

Making Anal Play
Good, Clean, Fun

3.1 Hygiene ~
Making the pleasure zones delicious
and safe for ultimate delight

One of the reasons women and men do not engage in anal play is because of the hygiene factor. Women are afraid that the area might not be fully clean, and men might have the same concern. I will cover how good hygiene for anal play can be attained in a fun and pleasurable way. To engage in anal play, both partners have to feel comfortable and know that the area is clean, safe, and ready for play.

You can make the act of cleaning the area and the gem a pleasurable, intimate, and erotic experience. Here's my method of cleansing. Let's say your woman now enjoys your fingers caressing around her gem and a little bit inside from the tongue play of Night 2. The next time you two are going to have fun, I would suggest taking a shower or bath together first. Make a sensual experience out of it. Light candles and have good sensual music. You can start with a bath to relax, and then turn on the shower. I will start with a shower example. Have fun soaping each other up and down. Lather her sensually, kissing her and caressing her body with liquid soap. Lather your chest thoroughly, and then lather her up her breasts with your chest. Use antibacterial soap to lather the lower half of her stomach all the way down and around to the top of her gem.

The cleansing process offers another chance to delight her with pleasure. Warm, soapy water feels really good when it is being caressed on your erogenous zones or on any part of you. Work up a lather, then start with her front. Turn her, so your chest is lathering her back, and you are caressing her breasts, stomach, thighs, and everywhere in between. Kiss her neck, and if she likes biting, bite the area between her neck and shoulder, gently, but deeply. You know what turns her on, so do what she enjoys. If you are not into sensual biting, I recommend you try it. It transfers a lot of intensely erotic energy.

Sensually move your hand and fingers to caress and play with her pussy. After some of this play, stand to her side, lather both of your hands, and start caressing and washing her back side and her front side. Have your fingers meet in the middle and play back and forth to wash her. Put Balneol Lotion (see back of chapter) on your pinky finger to wash the middle of her gem. See if you can push in lightly. First just put a little pressure on the outside of her gem, so you can feel good about licking her there later.

You can try to go in just a little and not past your nail. Remember, you are not trying to penetrate her yet, just wash her.

You will penetrate her gem more after Night 3, once she is comfortable with your finger going in her. Then you will take small steps: first up to the knuckle of your pinky, then to the next knuckle, as you get her to enjoy finger play. Make sure your fingers are well

3.1

manicured, filed, with no sharp hangnails. Make small circles with your pinky in her gem. If she feels good with that, try very slowly to go the second knuckle. If you have a thick pinky, try her pinky first. After she is used to anal play, you will be able to put in your whole pinky, then increase to your ring finger, and then with time, your middle finger [**See Image 3.1**].

Once she is comfortable with anal play, and you are able to go deep into her gem, then it is a good idea for her to start going to the bathroom beforehand to clear herself, followed by the shower scene above. Or, if you do not have a chance to take a shower together, then ask her in a sexy manner if she will clean herself with Balneol Lotion or antibacterial baby wipes when she is washing up for you, because you want to indulge in licking her pussy and all over for a long time. As her comfort with anal play increases, you can ask her to put her pinky inside, because you will be licking her gem intimately.

The next step in the process is to pleasure her around her gem and then inside her gem with toys. Cleanliness is definitely a very important part of anal play. If she is confident that she is clean, and she knows that you know that she is fully clean, then you can completely enjoy gem play and feel good about the hygiene factor.

The same goes for the man. If you want her to lick your gem, then you should shave and clean yourself for her to lick you. You want to make it pleasurable for her to pleasure you. Check yourself to make sure you smell good under your balls and your ass. Get a lotion or oil that smells good and tastes good, or has no taste, but make sure you smell good and taste clean. **Products I recommend are Hempz Original Herbal Moisturizer, Hempz Supre Pomegranate Lotion, Hempz Body Butter, Proclaim Professional Care Natural 7 Oils, and Making Love Massage Oil, Strawberries and Champagne.** All are available at a discounted price through EroticFlow.com. You want her to yearn for you to lick her, and for her to lick you. Then you two can enjoy a gem 69.

3.2 Clean Up for Anal Play

You can use an anal douche bulb filled with warm water to flush out the area. This helps later to greatly reduce the chance of anything coming out when you enter the gem with toys or your cock. There are anal douche bulbs you can buy on the Internet, or you can go to your local drug store and buy an anal douche bottle for three dollars. Make sure you get the bottle with the largest capacity.

Do not use the contents; empty it, and use slightly warm water, not hot. Read the bottle instructions, and use lubricant to make it easier to insert.

Once you and your partner are into having anal sex regularly, there are stronger options for cleansing, like the traditional red enema bag and shower attachments that will do a stronger cleaning. Again, with shower attachments, be sure to watch the water temperature. You don't want it hot; slightly warm is fine. With the red bag, read the directions carefully. Do not raise the bag up fast and high, or you will have a tidal wave of water going in the bum fast and furious. A possible shower attachment you can use is the Universal Water Works System; visit EroticFlow.com for where to buy.

One of the most thorough cleansing systems that a woman can use to make sure she is completely ready for hot anal sex is:

1. Use glycerin suppositories (you can get these at any drug store chain). Don't leave the house until you get the urge to go to the bathroom.

2. An hour or so after you use the suppository, use an anal douche as instructed above, and hold it in for as long as you can. Do this step twice.

3. Then use unscented baby wipes with **Balneol Hygienic Cleansing Lotion** to deeply wipe and cleanse the genitals and anal area.

4. Take a shower and rinse the area and your gem well with your finger. Then you will be good to go.

5. If some time passes before you actually start the fun do a baby wipe swipe right before to make sure you are clean.

3.3 Other Hygiene and Health Considerations

As I stated in Chapter 2, my purpose with this book is not to replicate what other resources have done well on topics of anal sex. My purpose is to document and illustrate in detail a step-by-step process that helps a woman go from being hesitant about anal play to LOVING anal play and anal sex. My method provides information on the timing to use for anal sex introduction techniques and a specific set of activities for each night in the system. My method enables anal play to progress pleasurably for both partners. There are resources on the Internet that offer good information of explaining anal health issues, and they can provide more in-depth content on this subject.

Go to the **Reseources Section** of this book and find **sub-section Anal Sex Health Research**. There I provide a variety of links to more in-depth research on anal sex health, anal anatomy, and anal sex Q&A articles published by medical and information websites.

As pleasurable as anal play and gem licking can be, you have to put in the time to learn about all the aspects of gem licking. If you are going to thoroughly lick her, you have to make cleanliness a must. If you don't, it can possibly lead to health issues. There are good books and websites on the subject of health issues that one needs to consider when engaging in anal play and gem licking (otherwise known as "rimming"). Millions of couples use good cleanliness, enjoy anal sexuality, and are fine. You need to do the research yourself to ensure you understand how to be safe. Also, when you are engaged in full-on anal sex and discover that a little fecal matter has made a surprise appearance, know this: it's no big deal. Just clean it off with a baby wipe. It is the human body; make sure that you make your woman feel comfortable, and that it is no problem at all. Reassure her that it is alright and that she does not need to feel embarrassed.

Another aspect in hygiene is fingernails. Make sure you cut your nails and file them, so they are very smooth. The gem is very sensitive to little edges and hangnails, so do a good job and test your nails on yourself. If you feel the edges, she will also. You can also use finger condoms. They are little, finger-size condoms that help prevent your nails from scratching her gem internally.

One very important point clearly made in all the books on anal play, and which must be reiterated here, is that you should not go from playing "in" her gem back to her pussy area with anything (this includes fingers, toys, and your cock). You should not finger her ass and then use the same finger to play with her clitoris or the outside of her pussy or the top of the area of her urinary opening. If you are using your hand to massage the area around her gem while you are going in and out of her gem, and your fingers are touching your cock, do not use the same hand/fingers to play with her clitoris. You can use finger condoms or latex gloves while you are playing with her gem area, and take them off to play with her clitoris. If she fingers her own ass or yours, she should not play with her pussy. **You can go from pussy to gem, but you cannot go from gem back to pussy.** You can clean your fingers with soap and water, then rinse thoroughly. Or clean your hands with anti-bacterial wipes. Use unscented baby wipes for wiping genital areas, but make sure the wipes do not have irritants.

If she goes through a thorough cleansing routine, you can play with less risk of mishap. I recommend designating one hand for gem play and the other hand for clitoris and pussy play. Thousands of people enjoy anal sex without any health issues—you can too! The content in this book does not guarantee safety, it is my best practices for providing a safer experience. Accidents can happen, like a condom breaking. Go to the Anal Sex Health Research sub-section to learn more on cleaning and safety from others.

I would also recommend wearing a condom the first several times you try anal sex with someone who is new to anal, until she is really well versed in a thorough cleansing process. Once she has done anal enough times for your entry to go smoothly, then it is up to you to consider going in without a condom. Do your research on the health risks before making your decision.

3.4 Toys for Explosive Anal Orgasms ~ Making the process completely pleasurable

You can give her incredibly explosive anal orgasms and make the process painless with the right use of toys. Toys are an important part of making the process of anal play orgasmic for her, so she loves it and yearns for it! You will love that she loves it, so it is worth spending the money for the right toys, lubes, and whatever else it takes to make this an amazing experience for both of you.

To get a woman to enjoy the process of gem play, you will need a toy with the right shape. The perfect toy is one that starts very small in the beginning and gradually gets bigger in girth, is made of soft, smooth material that is safe for anal play, and has the option to vibrate. This type of vibrator is surprisingly hard to find. A variety of sex stores both on the street and online do not carry this type of vibrator. After extensive research, I found some toy options that provide lots of pleasure and help her enjoy the eroticism of a toy stimulating her gem.

There are two types of stimulation that you need to do on her, so that the process feels good at all times. The first is using a toy to stimulate her clitoris and pussy. The second is using a stimulating toy to enter her gem. The first can be a normal vibrator, but it is preferable to have one with variable speed settings, so that you or she can set the vibration to a speed and power that feels exceptional to her. The second toy for her gem will be the type of toy I described a moment ago, starting small and gradually increasing in girth. There are a large variety of anal toys on the market; I am going to focus on the ones that are intended for a beginner and for incorporating erotic anal play into your sex life. As always, my focus is on making the process pleasurable.

Below are toys and lubricants that I recommend for pleasurably introducing a woman to anal play. Throughout this book I will describe when and how to use them. You can buy them through EroticFlow. com, where you will receive a discounted price. Also, EroticFlow.com will donate a percentage of the proceeds to charities chosen by its customers.

If you do not have a butt plug or a mini vibrator, then the product I recommend you start with is a **Vibrating Plug [See Image 3.2]**.

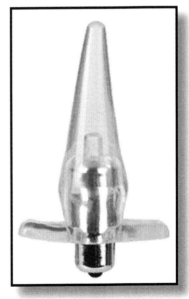

It is a smaller version of the ideal description I recommended earlier for a beginner toy. It starts small and gets bigger, it is soft, and it vibrates. Internet description: "A silicone butt plug with a vibrating bullet will have you smiling from cheek to cheek. Slip the waterproof, wireless, vibrating bullet into the soft silicone plug to relax muscles and provide extra stimulation, or slide it out to set your other pleasure points abuzz. It is silicone, so it is safe for anal play." This is a good starter toy.

3.2

3.3

The perfect toy would be a longer version of this one, so that the increase in girth is more gradual, goes to a bigger girth smoothly, and has a more powerful vibration design. But this product is close.

If you already have a mini-vibrator, you can get the **Anal Plug without the Bullet [See Image 3.3]**, which has an area to insert your mini-vibrator. Internet description: "With a silky texture, comfortable and sleek appearance and ability to warm quickly to your body. Designed for you to experience the true delight and enjoyment of adult toys! It has an insertable length of 3½ inches and a base width of 1¼ inches."

The **Twist Anal Vibe [See Image 3.4]** is perfect for the anal novice. The Twist will allow you to go where you haven't gone before. The easy-to-clean material and friendly size make it a great option for those new to anal play—it's totally non-intimidating. This toy does not rotate; it vibrates only.

Internet description: "Measures 9-inch total length, including battery compartment; Product Details: Speed: Variable; Material: Vinyl; Dimensions: 9-inches long x ½-inch wide; dildo length: 6 ½-inches long x 2-inches around; Batteries: 3 AAA, not included."

A toy that comes close to being the ideal toy is called the **Tingle Tip Vibe [See Image 3.5]**. This vibrator is almost perfect, except that it is not fully smooth, but it's close enough. Warning: this toy does not have a flared base like a plug, so you will need to make sure you do not try to insert the whole toy. Use the cord to wrap around your finger or around your wrist, so you can prevent it from going all the way in. What I like about this toy is that it starts small and gradually adds a good amount of girth over a longer length. This multi-speed wand massager has vibrations from

3.4

the tip to the back because of a small bullet in the front. Internet description: "Multi-speed wand massager with power tip gives focused sensations and vibrations. Flexible with a nubbed surface and a powerful bullet tip that concentrates on special spots and hang cord."

You can also use a beginner dilation set called the **Berman Dilator Set [See Image 3.6]**. It is a set of vibrators starting from a small girth to large girth. If you have a very thick and long cock, you should get this set. I like using this set because the design of the handle prevents the toy from going all the way in. Internet description: "This vibe is four vibes in one (think: Russian Nesting Dolls!). Designed to help with dilation, this vibe is great for those who may have medical reasons for wanting a versatile toy with graduating sizes. What's different about this dilator is its powerful multi-speed vibrations, adding more pleasure to the mix. With interchangeable, interlocking sizes, this hard plastic vibe is comfortable and smooth to insert. The set includes four sizes (3 ½" x 7/8", 4 ¼" x 1", 5 ½" x 1 ¼", 6 ¼" x 1 ½") and one silicone-blend sleeve that fits the smaller sizes.

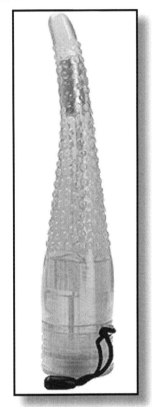

3.5

The silicone-blend sleeve is slightly porous; it is recommended to use condoms over this toy when the nubbed sleeve is being used, as it is the only way to keep it clean and bacteria-free."

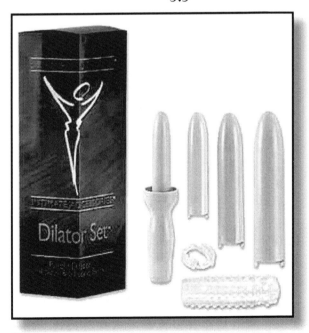

3.6

44

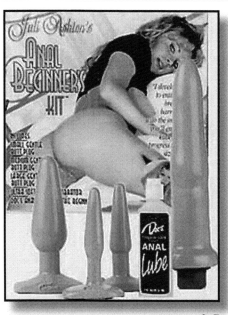

3.7

Here is another dilator set that uses butt plugs instead of vibrators, but only one component in this set vibrates, so I prefer the set that fully vibrates. The benefit with butt plugs is that they are made from softer material. If money is no object, get both. It is called the **Juli Ashton Anal Beginners Kit [See Image 3.7]**. Internet description: "Take your anal training to the next level with Juli's fun kit! This grab-bag of anal essentials will have you enjoying backdoor action in no time... Whether you're an experienced anal enthusiast or haven't ever tried this style of lovemaking before, this kit is ideal for all levels of sensual play. Includes 3 soft and flexible plugs: 4.25 x 1", 4.75 x 1", 5 x 1.5", and a multi-speed 7 x 1.5" vibrator for advanced stimulation."

3.8

Beaded toys provide a unique type of pleasure, and you can get one that does not vibrate or one that does. The ones that do not vibrate are usually longer and provide more stimulation when pulling them out during orgasms. Sample **Silicone Beads [See Image 3.8]**. Internet description: "This high-quality material is smooth and soft; these beads are graduated, so you can start slowly and have fun working your way up."

The next type of beaded toy is a vibrating one for additional stimulation. Vibration is amazing for making many things feel good. The nice feature of beaded toys is that they can stay in the gem at the different curved beads along the way. This toy is called **Spectra Gels Beaded Anal Vibe [See Image 3.9]**. With this toy you

3.9

can get her used to different levels of girth. Internet description: "Beginners will appreciate this toy's soft and forgiving material. The jelly sleeve houses a powerful yet quiet vibrator. The Spectra Gels Beaded Anal Vibe makes the jelly vibrate in the most soothing yet stimulating way imaginable. The beads gradually increase in size from top to bottom. The first three beads are flexible and are about the width of a normal-sized adult index finger. The Spectra Gels Beaded Anal Vibe handle is specifically designed for easy insertion and removal. To alter the vibration intensity, simply turn the cap at the base of the toy. Try taking this toy in the shower—its waterproof!"

Another toy for later in the process is called the **Spectra Gels Anal Toy [See Image 3.10]**. As the toy goes in the gem to the second curvature in the toy, it can stay in her gem while it vibrates, so the gem can get used to being consistently spread at a bigger girth while having vibration stimulation. You can then do other things to pleasure her while she enjoys the toy. Internet description: "Made from the legendary Spectra Gels rubber, this is one of the most popular materials on the market today. The Spectra Gels Anal Toy is soft to the touch, yet firm enough to stay rigid while in use.

3.10

This consistency makes this anal probe and Spectra gels the ideal choice for anal toys. This toy features a graduated and beaded shaft with full multi-speed vibrations."

You should purchase a good powered vibrator for her pussy, clitoris, and everywhere play. I like a **Slim Vibe [See Image 3.11]**. It is both versatile and powerful. Description: "Waterproof, with a powerful motor and a stylish metallic

3.11

finish. Slim, smooth, comfortable, and multi-speed! Great beginner toy, typically 6" long, 1" in diameter."

Last but not least, the toy used in the Body Quake position in chapter 5, the **Hitachi Magic Wand Massager [See Image 3.12]**, or a similar massager that will leave a long-lasting, full-body smile on your woman. This massager consistently receives five stars in customer reviews! Internet

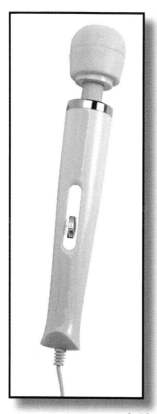

description: "It has a soft, spherical head and gives a soothing massage. It is operated by a two-speed switch located on the Wand's slender handle. Unlike cordless-style massagers, the Magic Wand's strong electric motor is powered using a standard electrical cord, providing a constant power source for those extended massage sessions." Two speeds: 1. "That feels so good," and 2. "OMG, I'm cumming," she screams!

Toys are an important part of the process for introducing a woman to anal sex. First, a toy should start very small and be exceptionally smooth, so that it is be comfortable for the woman. Second, stimulating her clitoris while engaging in anal play and entering her gem will allow her to enjoy the process more and cum throughout the process. Third, always wash your toys well with toy cleanser before and after you use them. I will go in-depth on what toys to use and how to use them as I continue to explain the process. But first, I will cover lubricants.

3.12

3.5 Lubricants ~
Enabling wetness to take her to new worlds of pleasure

Lubricants are the magic potions that enable you to bring her to new heights of ecstasy. There are many types of lubricants. Finding the right one will take some experimentation because taste or feel is a matter of preference. I tested a variety of lubricants to develop my assessment. I will explain the different kinds, provide my preferences, and give you a few options.

I want several benefits from my lubricant. First, the consistency has to be right: not too oily, not too thick, because it will feel like you are putting goo on her. It should not be too thin and watery either because they usually do not lubricate for a long enough time. I like for a lubricant to feel like an extension of her wetness. It might be slightly thicker when you put it onto your fingers, but once you massage it around, it should feel close to her wetness, or only slightly thicker in order to maintain lubrication for lots of motion.

Second, it should taste good enough to lick. It does not have to be sweet, but good enough for you to really indulge in kissing her, sucking her, and licking her for a long time.

Third, the dispenser needs to be convenient and functionally reliable. Get a dispenser that is small enough for you to work with one hand. Or get one with a system that lets you dispense easily and which you can easily have next to you on the bed. Not a big Costco bottle, but a dispenser that looks cool, not too big, and not so small that you could misplace it, but a size that remains functional. You want to have it conveniently next to you for efficient reapplication throughout the process.

I started with Astroglide for sex because I liked the consistency. Then I had a girlfriend who was irritated by the glycerin in it. So I tried silicone-based lubricants because they are supposed to last longer with smaller amounts. After trying Eros, which supposedly has a big following, I found I did not like the consistency of the lubricant. It was too thick and it felt oily. Those two products represent the two types of lubricants available: oil/silicone-based lubricants, and water-based lubricants. The water-based lubricants come with and without glycerin, flavored, and in cream form. I will focus on the water-based lubricants because I like the consistency better for anal sex. Water-based lubricants do not damage condoms, and they clean off the body and fabrics more easily than oil-based lubes. Oil-based lubricants, on the other hand, can negatively affect the condom material.

Water-based lubricants are available in several general consistencies. Thin and almost like water, medium consistency (this is my preference), thick like goo, or a thick sun-block. Thicker lubricants are said to be better for anal play, since a thicker lubricant can create an extra cushion of comfort for anal play and stay in place better, though I still prefer the medium consistency lubricant. As I stated earlier, I like a lubricant that is like a woman's own lubrication or slightly thicker. I also like that the medium consistency lubes spread more easily for a slip and slide effect. It feels good to the woman and to me when I use a lubricant that feels like an extension of her. Some of the thicker lubricants can be messier and/or stringier. Some people think that a thinner lubricant is cleaner, but I do not like a thin lubricant because it does not provide enough long-lasting lubrication for long sex interludes of several or more hours. Also, beware of when lubricants dry—some are more flaky than others. **My preferences are the following lubricants with medium consistency:**

1. **Please Liquid** – Glycerin free, great consistency, taste is decent to good. Not as good as a flavored lubricant, but good enough to lick for a long time. Con: when Please dries it is flaky. If you have dark bed covers or sheets and it gets on them, it will dry like a white flaky substance [**See Image 3.13**].

3.13

2. **Sliquid-Sassy** – Glycerin free, great consistency, there is no taste so it does not taste bad [**See Image 3.14**].

3.14

3.15

3. **Astroglide** (with glycerin) – This is my favorite. I like the consistency, not too thick, and not too thin. You can feel every groove of her anatomy and she can feel every groove of you better

3.16

than with silicone-based lubricants. It is not flaky and tastes fine. The glycerin free version does not taste good to me [**See Image 3.15**].

4. **ID Lube** (with glycerin) – Great consistency, tastes good, but make sure your partner is not prone to yeast infections if you use the glycerin types [**See Image 3.16**].

So now you have two options in the glycerin-free category and two in the glycerin category.

Item	Glycerin	Consistency	Taste	General comments
Please Liquid	no	great	decent	dries very flaky
Sliquid-Sassy	no	great	no taste	recommended for a glycerin free option
Astroglide	yes	great	good	if glycerin is not a problem for your woman, my choice, see site for updates
ID Lube	yes	great	good	can cause yeast infections but second best tasting

Flavored lubricants are good for oral sex and are not recommend for vaginal intercourse or anal. The sugar content used to make them taste good could lead to yeast infections. They can be stickier because of the sugar, and they are not recommended for anal. They are great if you are going to lick your woman for a long time on her pussy, or her gem, and if she is going to do the same to your cock, balls, and ass. If you are using a condom and you take it off for her to give you head, the flavored lubricant can help take away the taste of the condom. There are two types: flavored made from glycerin and made from Aspartame. There are many different flavors, so the flavor choice is a preference decision. **My recommendation for flavored lubricants:**

1. **Wet Flavored Intimacy Gel** – Kiwi-Strawberry – sugar free and non staining **[See Image 3.17]**.

2. **Sliquid Swirl** – Green Apple and Piña Colada **[See Image 3.18]**.

3.17

3.18

Below are options for other lubricants that you can try.

Thick water-based lubricants:

1. **Please Gel** – Glycerin free and thicker than Please Liquid.
2. **Slippery Stuff** – Glycerin free and about the same consistency as Please Gel, but it can be stringy.

Medium consistency water-based lubricants:

1. **Astroglide** – Glycerin and PABA Free – Nice consistency but I do not like the taste. You can taste for yourself at a Good Vibrations or buy sample packs from a store.

Thin water-based lubricants:

1. **Sliquid H2O** – Thin consistency and tastes okay.
2. **Pink Water** – Thinner, but I did not like the taste.

Cream Type Lubricants – I do not like the way creams look when applied or their consistency but you can try them and test them for yourself.

Cream Glycerin Lubricants:

1. JO H20 – Feels like a silicone lubricant but tastes better.

2. O My Natural Lube – Thicker than I prefer and does not taste that good

In chapter 4 you will discover exactly how to lubricate her gem to enable smooth entry. One of the tools that can be used to lubricate her gem for anal sex is an **Anal Lube Shooter** [See Image 3.19].

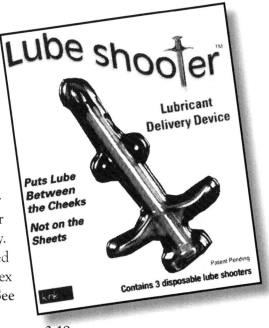

3.19

3.20

You can also use **Balneol Hygienic Cleansing Lotion** to clean after anal sex. It is soothing and meant for genital cleansing [See Image 3.20]. Use an "Adult Toy Cleaner/Cleanser" to clean your toys before and after use. Visit EroticFlow.com for which and where to buy. Now that you know some techniques on how to make anal play good, clean, and fun, you can enjoy the chapters to come. They will provide lots of pleasure to you and your lover.

Go to EroticFlow.com for new information on lubricants, toys and more. New studies come out all the time so it is important to stay informed. Go to Erotic Soul > Erotic Information.

Chapter Summary

Chapter Three ~ Prepare for Pleasure ~
Making Anal Play Good Clean Fun

3.1 Hygiene ~
Making the pleasure zones delicious and safe for ultimate delight

a. Address the concern of cleanliness of anal play by having a fun and sensual way to clean her and you before you play.

b. Take a shower together, create the mood in the shower, light some candles, play some music (you can find good erotic music on EroticFlow.com), and sensually clean her body and her gem. If you're only up to Night 2, clean on the outside and the center of her gem only. Slide ¼-inch of your fingertip in her gem to clean it, so you are good when you lick her. Tell her you want to lick her really well and want both of you to be really clean.

c. Once you complete Night 3, go in with a lightly soapy pinky finger to wash the inside of her gem. Rinse her really well with water to make sure all the soap is gone.

d. Once you have completed Night 4, you can go in deeper with your middle finger and do as item (c.) above suggests.

e. You should shave yourself and wash yourself properly if you want her to massage or lick you. It is only fair that you make it a nice experience for her. You would not want to lick a hairy ass, so don't make her do it.

There is more of a chance for things to stay around on hair.

f. Make sure you and she smell good; use a lotion or oil that leaves you smelling really good. Great products for smelling great are available on EroticFlow.com for a discount.

g. Cleaning system

  i. Use glycerin suppositories (you can get these at any drug store); don't leave the house until you get the urge to go to the bathroom.

  ii. An hour or so after you use the suppository use an anal douche. Hold on for as long as you can. Do this step twice.

  iii. Then use unscented baby wipes to clean deeply.

  iv. Take a shower, soap the area and your gem with your finger, then you are good to go.

  v. If some time passes before you actually start the fun, do a swipe with a baby wipe to make sure you are okay.

h. Get well educated on anal sex health

  The Ultimate Guide to Anal Sex for Women, 2nd edition, by Tristan Taormino and *Anal Pleasure & Health, a Guide for Men and Women* by Jack Morin, Ph.D

i. It is vital to repeat a very important point that is clearly made in all the books on anal play, and that is you should not go from playing in her ass directly to her pussy with anything—fingers, toys, or your cock. You should not finger her ass and then play with her clitoris or on the outside her pussy with that finger because there's a chance you can give her a UTI if you play on top of the area of her urinary opening.

3.2 *Toys for explosive anal orgasms ~*
Making the process completely pleasurable

a. Get the right toys to make anal sexuality (anal play & sex) extremely pleasurable and a painless process.

b. You will need two types of toys: toy/s for her clitoris and pussy, and toys for her gem.

c. The toys for her gem will have a safety system, so that they cannot be lost in the gem. There will be some sort of stopper or string that goes around your wrist.

d. Use a Vibrating Plug, The Tingle Tip, and the Berman Dilator when beginning to pleasure her gem. You can also use the other toys suggested for a variety of different pleasures.

e. You can use the Slim Vibe for pleasuring her clitoris and pussy.

f. Always wash the toys with cleaner before and after play.

3.3 *Lubricants ~*
Enabling wetness to take her to new worlds of pleasure

a. Using a good lubricant is imperative to anal play and to getting her to enjoy the process.

b. The right consistency and taste is important. Also, find out if she is allergic to sugars. You need to know this in case a lube with no glycerin or PABA is needed.

c. After testing and tasting a wide variety of lubricants, my favorite is an industry champion, Astroglide.

d. If she is not allergic to glycerin, you can use flavored lubricants on her and yourself to enjoy gem licking.

Cream Glycerin Lubricants:

1. **JO H20** – Feels like a silicone lubricant but tastes better.
2. **O My Natural Lube** – Thicker than I prefer and does not taste that good.

In chapter 4 you will discover exactly how to lubricate her gem to enable smooth entry. One of the tools that you use to lubricate her gem for anal sex is an **Anal Lube Shooter**.

You can also use **Balneol Hygienic Cleansing Lotion** to clean after anal sex. It is soothing and meant for genital cleansing. Use an "Adult Toy Cleaner/ Cleanser" to wash toys. Visit EroticFlow.com for where to buy. Now that you know some techniques on how to make anal play good, clean, and fun, enjoy the chapters to come, they will provide lots of pleasure to you and your lover.

A special note on silicone lubricants for anal sex. Some people online mention that they use silicone lube for anal sex and recommend it. For the introduction phase, I still recommend a water-based lubricant because you can feel more with it. Reapplying the lubricant frequently is also soothing to her gem during the beginning phase. You can test it for yourself, buy a silicone lube and a water-based lube and see which provides more sensation. After you enjoy anal sex frequently you can see which you would like to use long-term. I still prefer the water-based lube because of the amount of hand and finger techniques I add during anal sex. I like the way it feels. I would love your feedback on your experience. Go to the Resources section to learn how to provide your feedback and get rewarded.

Coming soon: Erotic Flow's first toy for couples and adult toy accessories for making vibrations even more pleasurable! Look for the EF emblem.

Chapter Four
Seduction Philosophy

Enjoy the Process of Pleasuring Her and Give Her Thrilling Orgasms Every Little Step of the Way

4.1 Body Seduction

The strategy to get her from curiosity to fulfillment, or from NO to Oh My God, that was AMAZING, is to convince her body and her mind simultaneously while leading her body to take the first small step. If you are with someone who is worth your time, then patience will not be much of a problem. This is a proven method to get women to try and enjoy anal play. By gauging where she is in terms of interest, previous experimentation, and how eager she is to try it, if at all, you can determine how to pace yourself and what to do, as I covered in the discussion on assessment in chapter 2. Here, I will start with the scenario of a woman who has never tried anal, is scared of possible pain, and is therefore, not interested.

4.2 Patience is Pleasure

You will implement the SEPOR Method and the 7 Nights to Ecstasy System starting from Night 1. The 7 Nights is a baseline in terms of the amount of time you should take. If she needs longer, then take longer; no matter how long it takes, it is worth your patience. The process will be enjoyable and erotic for both of you. It is not about having pain before pleasure. It is multiple nights of great pleasure before immensely pleasurable ecstasy! The length of time enables you to build trust because you are only going to do something small at every step, so she is sure to receive pleasure from it. There is no need to have a big conversation about anal sex or for her to do breathing exercises to relax her sphincter (anal) muscles. There is no need to worry about jumping into the deep end of the pool because the only thing she will do on the first night is touch the water with her pinky toe at the shallow end.

All you are going to do the first night is massage around the gem. Then, give her a great orgasm while massaging her gem. Let her enjoy the experience, and wait for the next time to try the next step. The conversation about anal pleasure will naturally come up as the steps progress, typically by Night 3 or 4. Then, you state the method you are using or show her this book if you like. If she wants to hold back and only go as far as the activities of a certain Night, then you will just keep doing that step and keep doing it incredibly! Do that activity with all your passion for as many nights as she wants. Do it so that it turns her on so much, it drives her wild. Let her know you get off on her happiness and pleasure by doing that step alone. Women want to know that you get off on their bliss. Over time she will become more eager and want more if you are truly flowing with her. You can then progress to the next small step. It does not matter how long it takes because you are enjoying each other's sexuality and erotic creativity. If you become impatient and go too fast because you are too eager, the ride will be over! Enjoy the ride!

4.3 Set-up Ahead of Time to Be Smooth During

As you progress through the steps, you will want to have all your tools and toys ready. You want to smoothly progress through the stimulation, instead of having to take a break to get the lubricant and then take another break to get all the toys. Keep a cool-looking box or bag for these items beside your bed, allowing you to easily reach them when you need them. At each night of the process, you will need different toys. Plan accordingly to have them clean and set them up for easy access and cool display. Why do you need a cool box or bag for your toys? Because presentation is important. It is just like how guys dig it when girls wear lingerie—the wrapping adds to the arousal and interest.

I covered Night 1 and Night 2 early in the book, so that women reading this book could relax and look forward to the pleasure to come. That early discussion was designed to help open their minds, get them interested in reading more, and motivate them to implement the cleansing aspects of sexual play. The cleansing aspect is important to implement for Night 3 to Night 7. The following pages will provide a method for measuring the degree of pleasurable patience that is required for the process to be successful.

4.4 The Process in Detail, Nights 3 to 7 ~
How to perform every touch, lick, and caress to build intimacy and pleasure to make her body and mind want more.

In this section, I will cover the remaining nights in detail. This will serve two purposes. The first is to let you know exactly what to do, and you can add your own flavor to the process. The second purpose is to entice and seduce your woman into trying the system for the immense pleasure she and you will experience throughout the process, if she reads this book. So let's continue!

4.5 Night 3 ~
Triple her pleasure

Now that you have enabled her to enjoy Nights 1 and 2, she should have a good association with ass and gem play. To continue to Night 3, you want first to have completed the foreplay techniques of Nights 1 and 2, exciting her with finger play and licking her gem, putting her thoroughly in the mood. I will now continue from the end of Night 2. After sensuously arousing her entire body, lay her on her back, and start to lick her pussy and clitoris (this takes into account that you had already started doing it before). I will cover some cunnilingus techniques in this book. Visit EroticFlow.com for greater details on cunnilingus techniques that she will love.

As you enact the following techniques, do not view them as steps you have to perform to get to a goal. View them as art that you are creating with your woman. Your erotic soul is dancing with hers, except the dancing is the licking, kissing, caressing, and sucking. When you are dancing or playing music, the goal is not to reach the end of the song, it is the fulfillment that you experience in the moment. So kiss her, lick her, and seduce her mind, body, and soul. Do this by creating together and expressing with her the art of your erotic souls.

Start to play with her pussy lips and clitoris with your fingers. Do this softly and sensuously and make sure to get feedback on the exact style and pressure your woman likes. Play with her U-Spot [**See Image 4.1**]. The U-Spot is a small patch of sensitive erectile tissue located just above and on both sides of the urethral opening. It is absent just below the urethra, in the small area between the urethra and the vagina. Less well known than the clitoris, its erotic potential was only recently investigated by American clinical research workers. They found that if this region was gently caressed with the finger, the tongue, or the tip of the penis, there was an unexpectedly powerful erotic response (Heretical.com/miscella/g-spots.html). Start licking her pussy and clitoris, take your middle finger and start to insert it into her pussy, lick your finger, and sensually circle it around her lips softly as you go in. Imagine all your energy flowing to your tongue and to your fingers as you continue to lick her.

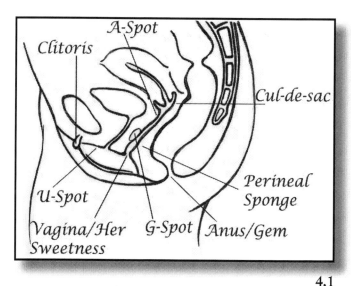

4.1

Take time to go all the way in and then push your finger to the bottom of her pussy, so you are applying some pressure to her bottom wall, the perineal sponge [**See Image 4.1**]. This stimulates her as well as lets her juices flow out of her more easily. Turn your finger up, so that the soft side of your finger is facing upward, and then bring your finger all the way up to the top of her pussy, the A-Spot. Play with the A-Spot (AFE-zone, or Anterior Fornix Erogenous Zone). Also referred to as the Epicentre, this is a patch of sensitive tissue at the inner end of the vaginal tube between the cervix and the bladder. It is the female equivalent of the male prostate, just as the clitoris is the female equivalent of the male penis. Direct stimulation of this spot can produce orgasmic contractions (Heretical.com/miscella/g-spots.html). Go in deep and sensually massage the top of her pussy. Bring your finger forward until you feel her G-Spot towards the front of her pussy, or about an inch or so inside with a slightly padded, bumpier texture on her skin (G-Spot receptiveness varies in all women. A good article was published in the LA Times, Health section titled "Mapping the Way to G-Spot Utopia," July 21, 2008) [See Image 4.1]. Once you get there, stimulate this area for a while, and play around passionately.

Next, lube your first finger thoroughly, and slowly insert it along with your middle finger into her pussy. When you go in, have your first finger massage her G-Spot. Massage it with a motion starting from the back and pulling toward you, as if you were telling someone to come to you in a sensual way. Put more pressure to see how much she likes on her G-Spot. Also, use both fingers to do the above and massage in circles as well. Then while your first finger is on her G-Spot, use your middle finger to massage the bottom area, the perineal sponge. The perineal sponge is erogenous tissue encompassing a large number of nerve endings, and can, therefore, be stimulated through the bottom wall of the vagina or the top wall of the rectum. Some women who experience orgasm during anal stimulation may be having their perineal sponge stimulated. These orgasms are often accompanied by ejaculation and are said to feel similar to orgasms that result from G-Spot stimulation (the-clitoris.com/f_html/female_ejaculation.htm).

Also pictured in Image 4.1 is the female Cul-De-Sac, an area I will cover later in this book. Play smoothly and softly, making sure you are fully lubricated as you play back and forth. Bring out as much of her juices as possible, so that she is dripping wet, and her juices are flowing down onto her gem. Her gem is now feeling the wetness from her pussy and your tongue. Take your other hand and start playing with your fingers around the inner area of her ass cheeks, around her gem. Massage her gem and the area around it. Then play with the outside of her gem with your pinky finger while you are simultaneously licking her and playing with two fingers inside of her pussy (use one or two fingers, whichever your woman prefers) [See Image 4.2].

4.2

As she starts to get more into the passion of the experience, circle your pinky around her gem, applying a little more pressure to arouse her, allowing more wetness to go into her gem. Again, start massaging gently from the center of her gem to massaging outward to help her skin stretch a little. This will serve two purposes. First, it will stimulate her. Second, it will help her gem adjust to being opened. Depending on your woman's lubrication, there might be enough lube all over your pinky. Try to go a little more into her gem. To be sure, have your little bottle of lubricant next to you, ready for you to squeeze some onto her pussy and gem.

Using small circles, apply light pressure while slowly inserting your finger into her highly-aroused gem. Both she and her gem will welcome more stimulation. Go in slowly and sensually to the first knuckle, pause a little until she gets comfortable. After about 30 seconds, wait for her to relax her sphincter muscles. (The interior sphincter is a muscular ring surrounding about 2.5 cm of the anal canal near the entrance that can be relaxed to open. The exterior sphincter is a flat plane of muscular fibers, elliptical in shape and on the outside of the internal sphincters and closer to the entrance of the anal canal. When both are relaxed, they can expand to let things through. More on the sphincter muscles can be found on the Internet).

Next, you rhythmically move in and out while slowly making small circles. Let all your passion come through on every lick and caress of your tongue; your passionate energy will transfer to her and make her feel very good. Gauge her level of stimulation and go in deeper with your pinky to the next knuckle, and wait for her to feel relaxed again before you go farther. Ask her how it feels. Getting verbal feedback along the way is important, and do so in a sexual manner. Remember, your nails should be well filed, or you can use a finger condom. You can also switch to one of the small butt plugs, which start smaller than your pinky and are totally smooth [**See Image 4.3**].

Continue stimulating her with your finger. If she says it feels good, then go in deeper with slow, sensual movement. Make sure you are fully lubricated before you go in farther. Keep your pinky still for a bit, wait for relaxation, then start with slow sensuous movement, so she can get used to the finger moving in and out. Turn your pinky so that the soft side is up. Massage the upper wall inside her gem, where you can feel your middle finger from your

4.3

other hand. Play so that both fingers are stimulating her wall. Go in all the way with your pinky and continue the play with the wall between her gem and pussy.

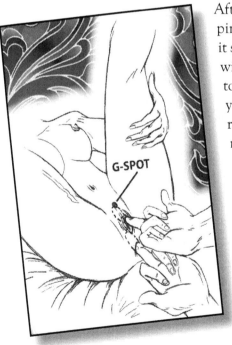

G-SPOT

4.4

After some play, switch from your pinky to your middle finger. Ask her if it still feels good as you enter her gem with your middle finger. Remember to reapply lubrication **every time** you switch fingers. Do not try to rush it. Take the time for your middle finger like you did for your pinky finger. All this time, you are still licking her and playing with her pussy with one or two fingers [**See Image 4.4**]. The advantage of fingers as opposed to a toy is that you can curve your fingers to provide variable internal stimulation. Your finger is warm, and it is more intimate. Toys do provide a smooth surface and vibration, but the intimacy factor is higher with your fingers. I enjoy using both, but I would suggest starting with your fingers if they do not bother her.

Using small circles, insert your middle finger into her hot and wanting gem, which is now enjoying some major stimulation. Go in slowly, one knuckle at a time. Continue to do circles, go in deeper and massage the top wall sensually, then all around. You can now start to alternate the sequence of penetration between your left and right hand. As one hand goes in to stimulate her pussy with two fingers, the other hand (finger) is coming out from her gem, and vice versa. While you are licking her clitoris, her U-spot, and all round her wet sweetness, send all your energy and every ounce of your soul to your lips, tongue, and fingers. [**See Image 4.5**]

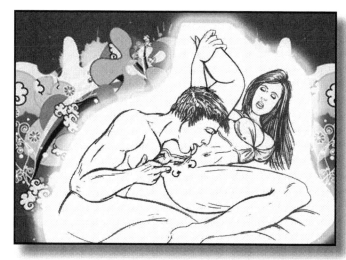

4.5

Then switch to entering her with both hands/fingers at the same time and going in deeply. As you do this, all your passion should be pouring out. That means you are every sensual bite, you are every suck, and you are every kiss. There is nothing else in your mind but the pleasure and connection you two are experiencing.

Your erotic soul should be flowing into every lick, every caress, and every insertion of your fingers. Hum and moan on her clit, getting feedback from her that she is still feeling good, and continue to arouse and excite her until she has to release into an explosive orgasm [**See Image 4.6**].

If you have the type of woman who can continue to receive stimulation during orgasm, then by all means continue. If her body becomes sensitive, then slow down or stop—but do not pull out suddenly because it will be very uncomfortable for her. Let her gem pulse and squeeze your finger as she cums for you. More fun activities during Night 3 are the techniques:

c. V-Spot Massage, h. CrissCross, l. Fingertips and w. U-Spot Love, which are covered in chapter 5, "**Erotic Anal Play – Delicious Stimulation for Both of You.**"

Then ask how she feels. See if she wants you to slowly pull your fingers out. If she has multiple orgasms, then see if you can give her another.

If not, then pull out slowly and let her enjoy her experience. You two can then continue with vaginal intercourse. Let this be it for this night. Let her enjoy the thoughts and emotions of an orgasm associated with

4.6

penetrative anal play. Let her relish the pleasure that will inspire her to continuously want more.

4.6 Night 4 ~

Vibrate her soul

In this night you will add a toy to help her enjoy thicker girth in her gem. Since Night 4 is a new night, you will go through the initial parts of Nights 1–3 to arouse her but not bring her to orgasm yet. Now that she is comfortable with a finger in her gem, you can step up the level of cleansing before play and have her do an anal flush with warm water. Have her do this for every following night.

Start where you have entered her gem with your middle finger, using small circles as in Night 3. Next, you are going to use a vibrating plug with a small starting girth that gradually grows in girth, either a Vibrating Plug or the Tingle Tip Vibe would be good. Remember, she is still on her

4.7

back, maintaining intimacy and sensual passion. Turn on the vibrator and begin to lightly stimulate her clitoris, her lips, and then the outer parts of her gem. Go up and down over her gem, and keep going in a circular motion, too. Next, lube the entire vibrator, and while you are simultaneously licking her and fingering her pussy, slowly insert the Vibrating Plug [**See Image 4.7**].

Ask her how it feels. Does she like the vibration? Then, continue to be conscious of when you reach the point on the plug where it is bigger than your middle finger because this will be a new girth for her. You should slow down and use small circles to guide the plug gradually to a bigger girth. Make sure she is enjoying the process. She will be if you are licking her and fingering her sweet pussy sensually with all that erotic energy flowing into her pussy.

IMPORTANT: Circling Techniques (CT) – the reason I suggest **using small circles while entering her gem** is because if you try to expand all sides of her gem at the same time by just pressing in, you will be stretching all sides at the same time. That will be uncomfortable and likely painful. If you use small circles, the motion expands and relaxes a side at a time, giving the skin a better method to adjust for eventually accepting you into her gem [**See Image 4.8**]. You are massaging, relaxing, and stimulating her as you insert a finger, a toy, and eventually your cock. As you circle you can press/pull gently in any direction for 2–3 seconds, then move to another direction and press/pull for 2–3 seconds and continue all the way around.

When making small circles slightly bigger than her gem, it should take 3–4 seconds to make a full sensuous circle. Do circles for at least 20 seconds to a minute, insert the toy a little more, and hold the Tingle Tip at the new girth for a little bit, so she can get used to the new girth. One hand should be holding the toy while the other is massaging the gem area around the

toy, and your tongue is licking her clitoris. Then, start to play with the toy, spin it, going in and out to the new girth and gradually increase the girth, using the same technique. The Tingle Tip is not too intimidating, so go as far as she is comfortable. Circle at least 20 seconds in place, then insert about an inch and pause for 20 seconds. Do this circling and timing strategy for every inch you enter. Next you will start alternating the sequence of entry with your fingers going in her pussy and the Tingle Tip in her gem. Keep doing that at the same time, and stimulate her G-Spot and A-Spot.

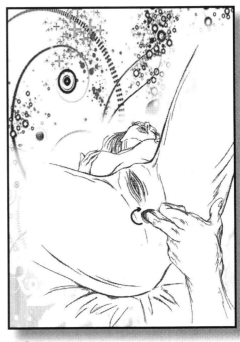

4.8

When you use a Vibrating Plug, it is shaped so you can go the end and leave it in while it is vibrating to stimulate her and get her used to a slightly bigger girth. With the Vibrating Plug in her gem, start to play with her pussy using your cock. Tease her entire beautiful pussy area until she is begging you to enter her pussy.

Then begin to enter her slowly to see how she feels with the plug in her gem while you are entering her pussy. This is going to feel incredible for you, too, because her pussy will be vibrating from the plug in her gem. Go in all the way, slowly and methodically, while playing with the plug in her gem. Once she is used to both your girth and the plug, thrust more passionately. Play with the plug as you are thrusting inside her; have the plug going in and out and twisting. Continue to lube the toy to make sure it moves smoothly. You can do this type of play in a variety of positions: missionary, side, doggy, and her riding you are just a few.

Now instead of the plug, insert two fingers in her gem using the same circling technique. Put your first finger over your middle finger, insert them sensually, and imagine sending energy to your fingers while you are licking her clitoris [**See Image 4.9**]. I will cover more specific technique details in the anal play positions section of this book.

4.9

Another way to get her used to a bigger girth is by switching to the smallest vibrator in the Dilator Set by Berman. This vibrator is thicker than your finger, smooth, and has a similar girth throughout the length of the vibrator. Lick her and insert your fingers in her pussy, then use the vibrator to play with her gem as you start inserting it using the circling technique. You now can take longer strokes with this vibrator as you pleasure her. Take the time to thoroughly pleasure her with this first size in the Berman System. Pour more lube on the vibrator and slowly take it out by doing circles on the way out and massaging the area around her gem.

Put on the second attachment of the Berman Dilator System. Start by pouring more lube on the area and all up and down the toy. Lick her, kiss her everywhere, and arouse her sensuality. You will now implement a new circling technique, called **Circling oooh OOOHs**. Start by making small circles, a circumference slightly wider than her gem, have the entire circle take about three seconds, and do about three of them. Now make wider circumference circles, but slower, so that it takes five seconds to do the full circle. Do three of these. Do three more small circles, then slowly push forward about an inch into her gem. Only push forward after you complete three small, three bigger, three small circles. Then you can enter slowly using small slow circles for about an inch. Hold for about 30 seconds and let her get used to the new girth. While you are holding, massage the skin area around her gem by twisting your hand around the toy on the area around her gem, while you are licking and sucking her clitoris passionately. Now pull back and go back and forth to the new depth you just reached, twisting the toy while you do so, licking her while you do so. Again, pour more lube on the toy and her gem area. Repeat everything in this paragraph to go in another inch. Then, do everything again until you get to about 3 inches or so inside. Play with the toy, spin it, go back and forth, and stimulate her senses. Talk sexy to her, tell her how beautiful she is, how much you love pleasuring her. Lick, kiss, and suck her pussy and clitoris with all your passion and soul. Then make her cum by licking and fingering her or by inserting your cock back in her pussy while you still play with the vibrator in her gem [**See Image 4.10**].

Let that be the amount of gem play for Night 4. Talk about the experience afterwards. Let her know how much it turned you on, and ask her what she liked, and what felt good. Ask about the speed of inserting the plug. Was it slow enough? Does she want it faster? And ask her to let you know when you are making her gem and ass feel really good as it is happening. Hot sexual communication about gem play during and after sex is an erotic experience. More fun activities during Night 4 are techniques: **a. The E3** [**image 5.2**], **d. V-Spot and Vibe Combo, k. Pearls,** and **u. Bend Over, Beautiful [image 5.32]**, covered in chapter 5.

4.10

4.7 Night 5 ~

Expand her ecstasy

Night 5 is going to be very similar to Night 4, except you are going to use a dilation system and other varieties of toys to add more stimulation and get her used to larger girths at a gradual pace. Soon, she will be used to the size of your girth. Night 5 may need to be repeated two or more times, depending on your woman and the size of your cock. It is important that you gradually pleasure her using small increments of increasing girth so that it does not hurt her, and so she keeps enjoying the process. Going too fast can lead to her stopping the process for that night or stopping it entirely. You don't want that! So take your time and enjoy the process because the rewards are so worth it.

You will use a dilation system that has either vibrators or plugs from small to big girth sizes. I prefer vibrators because they add more stimulation. You are also going to use the Tingle Tip Vibe to help you go smoothly from one dilation size to the next. Since the dilator vibrators jump from one size to another, the Tingle Tip will help transition her from one dilator to the next. Again, it is about making the increase in girth smooth, pleasurable, fun, and hot. I suggest using the Berman Center Dilator Set and the Tingle Tip Vibe. After Night 4, she should be used to the full girth of the Vibrating Plug toy. Again, follow the process of Nights 1 to 3 because you always want to lead her arousal, so that she is yearning to experience more.

Now that you have stimulated her, she is ready for gem play. While you lick her, play with the Tingle Tip on her clitoris, around her lips, her U-Spot, in her pussy, and down to her gem. Remember to fully lubricate her and the toy. Circle the toy around the gem and go inside. Slowly and very sensually go back and forth. Guide it to the girth that she reached on Night 4. Play around at that girth, use the circle technique, and then go in a little more. The Tingle Tip helps her adjust to increased girth because it starts small and goes to thick. To get her used to long strokes that are consistently bigger, you will switch to the first vibrator in the dilator set and play with the vibrator going in and out, twisting, doing small circles, simultaneously licking her and fingering her warm, wet pussy. This all should go smoothly because the size of the first vibrator is small, which is the size she had already experienced on Night 4.

You are now going to increase girth. Using the circling technique explained on Night 4, insert the Tingle Tip to just about the size of the 2nd attachment on the Berman dilator set (the second to last attachment).

Play with the Tingle Tip until she is used to the new size on the dilator set. Play as instructed earlier. Put on the 2nd attachment in the dilator set. Since this is a new and bigger girth all the way down the shaft, go in slowly using **Circling oooh OOOHs** and **Pleasure Twists** techniques (Pleasure Twists technique is also covered in chapter 5). There are five steps to doing Pleasure Twists:

1. Put your first finger and thumb around the front of the vibrator against her ass ring, the skin area around her gem. Use the side of your first finger all the way to your thumb to massage her ring by twisting your fingers sensually around the vibrator.

2. Put your thumb in her pussy so when you twist your hand around the vibrator, your thumb goes in and out of her pussy. Massage her tang and her perineal sponge during the back and forth movement of your thumb.

3. Use oooh OOOHs to gradually expand her gem in a pleasurable way and Circling (small circles) or push downward to insert, whichever she likes.

4. Use your other hand holding the back of the vibrator to turn the vibrator counter clockwise and clockwise, using the opposite direction than the massage you are doing with the top hand. Also, once you have entered her gem a bit, use this hand to move the vibrator back and forth in her gem, adding even more stimulation.

5. Lick, suck, and kiss her clitoris, U-spot, and labia so amazingly that she can't help but love your tongue and all the stimulation that is enabling the new vibrator to go in her gem. Do all the above while all your passion pours on to her, with moans, hot erotic energy, and hot sex talk [See Image 4.11].

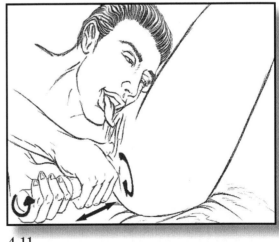

4.11

Continue to lick her pussy and clitoris passionately. Use the Circling oooh OOOHs technique explained on the second-to-last paragraph of Night 4 for every inch you go in. Use the circling, massaging, licking, pleasuring technique until you reach 4 inches or so with this attachment. Make her feel incredible,

talk to her, tell her how beautiful every part of her body is, how sweet her pussy is, how luscious her gem is, how sexy and hot she is, how much she turns you on, and play with her until she cums all over you [**See Image 4.12**].

4.12

Have this be it for Night 5, in terms of increasing size. You can continue anal play with this current size during this night, but wait until next time to do the next increase. So now you have taken her to the second size vibrator, the second to last in the set. If your cock is about this size, or a little bigger, then you can go on to Night 6. If you are much bigger in girth than the last dilator size, for example 2 inches wide, then you should do everything in Night 5 again during the next night and increase to the last size in the dilator set. Your patience will pay off by creating an intimate moment where the process is so incredibly pleasurable for her throughout all of it, she will not only love you for it, but she'll love to engage in anal play, and she will yearn for it.

If you are even bigger than 2 inches wide, then you are going to do the Night 5 process with a dildo or vibrator that is progressively closer to your girth. Devote one night for every new size until you get to something that is close to your girth. Reward and appreciate her for every new experience. Let her know how much it turns you on. Do something sweet to thank her for not only trying, but also for enjoying the process. Hold her afterwards. Remember, it is an intimate experience. Get her feedback to make sure she likes how you are doing things and if there are other things she wants you to do to her gem as well.

During Night 5, you can also use the silicone beads of an appropriate size [See Image 4.13]. At every new girth you take her to, you can then play with this toy to the bead that is the size of the new girth. Lube and play, back and forth, and twist it around. Then, insert the beads until they reach the new girth.

Leave it in so she gets used to the new girth; it will stay in place. Lube the beads, and play back and forth while you sensually

4.13

massage the area around her gem and all around her pussy. Play with her G-Spot, U-Spot, and A-Spot. Go in and out with the beads while licking and massaging. Have sex while the beads are in, and when she is cumming, pull the beads out of her gem. This will add to the pleasure of the orgasm. Tell her how much you enjoy licking her and playing with her clitoris, sweet pussy, and luscious gem at the same time. Play with the area around the gem while the beads are in and as she is pulling them out.

4.14

More fun activities during Night 5 are: **a. The E3, j. Good Vibes, and y. Body Quake** positions covered in chapter 5. Insert a vibrator in her pussy and another in her gem while you lick her clitoris. Circle the vibrators at the same time, in and out, in the same direction and in opposite direction [See Image 4.14].

"A girl can have anal orgasms while there is a good size cock in her gem, I have to see it to believe it!" is what a beautiful person said to me one time. After thinking about it, it made total sense. Of course, if girls do not regularly talk about anal sex, they are not sharing how they have or can have incredible orgasms from anal sex. So I searched the Internet for videos of women really enjoying anal sex and having explosive orgasms from anal sex. My research is on EroticFlow.com in the members section.

4.8 Night 6 ~

Entering the Gem of intimacy

YES, you are now at the stage where you have gradually taught to her enjoy anal play enough to have you enter her gem. By this time, she wants to feel the heat of your cock in her gem. And oh damn, does it feel good and look amazing! It is important that you implement the techniques in this section so as to avoid any pain for her. Remember to cleanse thoroughly and implement the cleansing method in the hygiene section of this book. Have the lubes and toys next to you. You should wear a condom this time

4.15

because your skin will absorb more lubricant than the rubber. If you are monogamous and without disease, you can read medical websites or the previously referenced books on general anal sex to decide if you want to later switch to not wearing a condom. You will do the arousal techniques of Nights 1–5 to get her really hot and ready for your cock.

Leave-In Technique: Get her ready for anal sex by leaving in an anal vibrator or plug that has a girth that is nearly the size of your cock. Leave it in for at least 3 to 5 minutes so her gem can get used to staying open for some time. Now that you are going into her gem, you want to maintain intimacy and pleasure. Lay her on her back.

Have her at the edge of the bed so that you are standing (enables more control), and then put a pillow under her ass to angle up her gem. You are going to stimulate her with your cock and hands to turn her on even more. Take the time to sensually enjoy this act. Lubricate her pussy, clitoris, and gem, so she is slippery. Use the head of your cock to play with her clitoris, pussy, and gem. Go everywhere with the head of your cock, in circles and in an up and down pattern [See Image 4.15].

4.16

Get creative and use your fingers. This can add pleasure to her multiple erogenous zones simultaneously. Remember her U-Spot? Dip inside her warm, wet pussy and tease it. Use your hand to play with her while at the same time your cock is massaging her [See Image 4.16]. Use the patterns on Images 4.17, 4.18, and 4.19 to play with her clitoris, pussy, tang, and gem. Simultaneously use both your hand and your cock to give her pleasure. While your hand is on her clitoris, your cock is on her gem, and vice versa. Have your cock start the pattern, and your hand can follow behind [See Images 4.17, 4.18, 4.19]. Since you are on the outside of her gem, you are not violating the no gem to pussy rule.

To lubricate her for Night 5, you are going to implement a technique I call **Waves of Lubrication**. This technique lubricates her gem in a hot and stimulating manner, thus preparing her to enjoy anal sexuality with your cock inside her warm, sweet, tight, and yearning gem. You are going to use the Beauty Beads Purple toy. Apply lots of lube on the toy, and sensually insert the first three or four bulbs. Pull them out, then push them back in several times. Again, generously lube the toy, and slide it in a little farther.

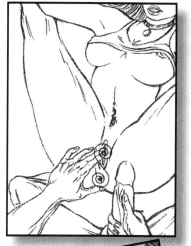

Slide it in and out, letting the generous amounts of lube lubricate the inside of her gem deeply. Go in as far as the length of your cock, or more, depending on how deep she enjoys it, so she is deeply lubricated and can take you in more easily when you start entering her gem of pleasure. You can also use the Anal Lube Shooter shown in chapter 3. When you apply lube to yourself, make sure you cover your cock's full length.

4.17

Then use a vibrator to play with her clitoris and pussy. I like the Slim Vibe, but you can use whatever vibrator she prefers. You are going to reapply lubricant to her pussy and her gem. Keep the vibrator on her clitoris, play with the head of your cock on her lips, in her pussy, and then go down to play with the head of your cock around her ass and gem.

4.18

Now you are going to implement the circling technique covered in Night 4. Grab yourself with your dominant hand, and put your thumb on top of your cock to provide good guidance [See Image 4.20]. Make circles sensually, gradually making them smaller around her gem. You are going to continue to make very small circles at the entrance of her gem while gradually applying pressure forward. Remember, in this night, you have already prepped her with a vibrator from the dilator set, so you are not going to be the first thing going inside her gem. You have gradually prepared her to take you, using the progressive steps you have made from previous nights. Also, implement the Pleasure Twists technique.

4.19

As you make the small, sensuous circles on her gem with your cock, use your thumb from the hand that is holding your cock to play with her pussy lips, and slide the thumb in and out of her pussy. Your other hand is holding and playing with the vibrator on her clitoris.

Or, she can hold the vibrator, and you can switch that hand to play with her nipples or around her pussy. Look into her eyes and tell her how beautiful and hot she is, how good she feels, how delicious her pussy and gem are. You are going to make small, slow circles until the head

4.20

of your cock goes into her gem. You can also try pulling/pushing gently to variety of directions, holding for 2 to 3 seconds at each point. Ask her what feels better. Pour more lubricant on top of your cock to the head and massage it all around your entire cock and around her gem, which is now wrapped around your head. Stay still and hold for 30 seconds to a minute while you do steps 1 and 2 of Pleasure Twists (Step 1: Massage the area around her gem with the side of your first finger to the bottom of your thumb. Step 2: Insert the thumb in her pussy and massage her perineal sponge and tang) [**See Image 4.21**].

If she still feels tight, you can try a technique I call the **Gem Relax Technique**. The two sphincter muscles in the gem have a protective response, and they just need to relax. If you tire out the muscles before you go in, the muscles will relax easier. Pull out slowly, and before you go back in, have her squeeze her gem and Kegel muscles as tightly as possible for 45 seconds. Rest for 10 seconds, then squeeze for another 45 seconds. Now her sphincter muscles are tired and will relax easier. Continue with the oooh OOOHs technique with the Pleasure Twists, and use your thumb to stimulate the pussy and tang.

4.21

Generously apply more lubricant to the area around her gem and to your entire cock. The hand grabbing your cock is going to continue to make small circles with your cock, sensually massaging the area around her gem as you slowly enter her gem. So, not only are you circling your cock to enter, but you are also twisting your hand around your cock to sensually massage the gem area while your thumb is stimulating her pussy and tang. Once you get your head in, continue doing Pleasure Twists massaging to stimulate the area around her gem with thumb massage. During this time, she is holding the vibrator on her clitoris, and your other hand is stimulating her nipples, mouth, or other erogenous zones. Yes, that is the most pleasurable multi-tasking you'll ever do. Don't feel rushed. Enjoy pleasuring her!

Enjoy the moment you are in. Talk to her with stimulating words; let your breath communicate your passion; and pay attention to her facial and body cues to assess your progress inward.

IMPORTANT: Do the **Circling and oooh OOOHs** techniques from Night 4 again. Do several small, three-second circles; several wider, five-second circles; and several small, three-second circles. Only then will you very slowly push forward for about an inch using slow, very small circles or push down your cock a little as you enter (see which she likes better). As you enter, she should only feel light pressure and not any pain at all. After entering about an inch, hold for about 30 seconds to let her get used to you. Kiss her sensually, look into her eyes, and talk to her passionately. Do Pleasure Twists while holding still, until she adjusts to you deeper. She has kept the vibrator right on her clitoris the whole time, so everything is feeling really good for her. Adjust the vibrations, so they feel just right. Direct clitoral stimulation can be too intense for some women, so have her place the vibrator where it feels best. (If the vibrations are too much, then you are going to have to do the stimulation with your thumb or fingers, but one way or another, keep the stimulation going on her clitoris.)

Make sure she feels okay and relaxed enough for you to continue. Move back and forth slowly and sensually while playing with her pussy and massaging around her gem. Pleasure her for two minutes or more while moving slowly back and forth and massaging with Pleasure Twists but you are not going farther than the inch you entered. You are just getting her to enjoy thoroughly the depth at which you are. Massage more lubricant around your cock and around her gem and do everything from the bolded "important" above for every inch or so that you enter. This will make every inch of you a smooth and good experience for her. To review, the circling technique above is part of the **Pleasure Twists** technique to enter her gem, so follow these **5 Steps to Enter Her Gem:**

1. Massage her ring area with the side of your first finger to the bottom of your thumb. Use your thumb to massage her pussy and tang as your hand turns.

2. Use the oooh OOOHs technique, do several small three-second circles, several wider five-second circles, and several small three-second circles again.

3. Enter an inch using small circles or by pushing your cock downward and pause for 30 seconds or so to let her adjust to you. Use Pleasure Twists while in pause mode, kiss her and use your free hand to arouse other erogenous zones. Stimulate her clitoris throughout the whole time with a vibrator (she can hold the vibrator [See Image 4.21]).

4. Go in and out slowly and sensually to the inch you have penetrated, not any further for a little while as you do more Pleasure Twists to arouse her. Pour more lube on her clitoris and gem. Use the hand dedicated to her pussy to massage her clitoris and your other hand to massage the lube sensually on her gem and your cock.

5. Repeat the above steps for every inch you enter. Kiss, lick, suck her wherever you can reach (her lips, neck, breasts, legs, feet, and toes) throughout the steps.

During all the above activities, your other hand was free to simultaneously play with her pussy, U-Spot, breasts, nipples, lips, and body. Your mouth was free to simultaneously kiss her legs, her toes, her calves, her nipples, her mouth and tongue. There should be multiple points of pleasure: her clitoris is being stimulated by the vibrator, the outer and inner pussy by your thumb, the ring area around her gem with the side of your finger/hand, her gem with the warmth of your cock, and—even more importantly—the depth of your connection through the intimacy of this experience. With practice you will be able to do all of the above actions simultaneously. Do sex talk that turns her on, while your shoulders, hips, and body wave sensually with your woman! Playing drums, playing guitar and singing, or engaging in other activities that help condition your body to do a variety of different things with each limb, enables you to do all the above simultaneously while you are in rhythm and in sync with the energy of your woman.

As you go in farther inside, feel your souls wrap around each other, breathe together, and flow together in that experience. If you love her, send your love or caring to her with every kiss. Send that energy to your fingers and send it to your cock. She will feel your emotions. The more physical and emotional pleasure you create, the more she will enjoy it. Once you have entered 2/3rds of your cock's length in her and you have been playing back and forth for a bit, put more lube on your cock and around her gem. Massage the lubricant around the gem; do not just place the lubricant there. Do it in a way that gives her more sensual stimulation around her gem, and make the entire circumference feel really good. You want to keep doing this throughout the process and throughout the time you are having anal sex. It keeps her gem well lubricated while adding stimulation.

You are going to keep the vibrator in place as you lean forward to kiss her breasts, look into her eyes, and kiss her passionately. Support yourself so you do not accidentally thrust inside of her while you are leaning forward. As you kiss her, let her know how good her gem feels wrapped around your cock, how good she feels wrapped around you, and how much she turns you on. Let your verbal play excite her even more. Continue inch by inch, massaging and entering, keeping stimulation to her clitoris, pussy, U-Spot, G-Spot, and gem. In this intimate and passionate position, you can use your hand instead of the vibrator to stimulate her clitoris [**See Image 4.22**].

Make sure she is enjoying every inch of the experience. Again, ask her what feels good. Does she want slower, faster, deeper? But you are not going to pump hard on Night 6—that is for Night 7. Night 6 is to get her to enjoy her first anal sex experience with your cock inside her gem. Remember, patience is pleasure. Massage her, and put more lubricant on and around her gem and your cock. Then, start to go back and forth slowly with longer strokes since most or all of your length is inside of her now. She can either still hold the vibrator or lay it between your bodies so it stays on her clit. You are still kissing her, biting her neck, licking her, and loving her.

Get feedback from her to see if it feels okay for you to go a little deeper and faster.

4.22

Guide the progression with continuous feedback, and make the dialogue HOT! You two are now engaged in a very hot, passionate, intimate, and erotic sexual experience. Tell her how good it looks to be inside her gem, and how hot and beautiful she is.

Remove the vibrator and put a lot of lubricant on your pelvic area, so when you are lying on her, your pelvic bone will stimulate her clitoris with the slip and slide effect of the lubricant. You are also going to reach around and put more lubricant around her gem while you are still inside. When lying close to her, reach around and massage her gem with your lubricated fingers as you go in and out of her so that you pleasure her gem from the outside with your fingers and the inside with your cock. The finger technique is as follows:

1. First finger massages the bottom side of her gem.

2. Middle finger massages her upper gem and her tang.

3. Ring and pinky fingers massage her clitoris and the inside and outside of her pussy [**See Image 4.23**].

4.23

If you are standing, massaging her gem with your lubricated fingers will also enable your cock to slide in and out easier.

Make sure you continue to use the vibrator while you are still sensually sliding in and out of her gem. You can also insert your fingers into her pussy to stimulate her (make sure it is not the same fingers that were playing with her gem). Do all the above until she has an explosive orgasm from you being inside her gem and receiving all the other pleasure at the same time. Give her a break afterwards, so she does not get too sore from her first time and has a good feeling afterwards. If your woman has multiple orgasms, then see how she feels and if she wants you to continue. If she does not have an orgasm within 30 minutes or so of anal sex, let that be it for this time. You don't want her to get sore from a lot of activity the first time you enter her. You want to leave her wanting more. If you have a big/thick cock that gets bigger towards the base and expands a lot from pulsating when you orgasm, then pull out slowly to just before the head of your cock before you orgasm. If you do not the circumference of your cock towards the base can expand too much during your orgasm and can hurt her on her first anal penetration experience. You do not want her to experience any pain so be thoughtful of her gem and gradually position your cock to where it does not expand so much.

When you are ready to come out, DO NOT PULL OUT FAST. Pour more lube on her gem. Do small circles and massage around her gem while you back out. Take your time and pull out slowly and carefully. She will be sensitive, so be smooth on the exit so that everything is a good experience. You want her to remember all the pleasure so that her memories of the experience drive her to want more. Remember to talk about the experience and get her feedback, so you can become a master of her pleasure in every way and of every part of her. You two are now able to continue expanding the amount of activity and positions you can do with anal sex. Night 7 will cover how to go deeper and faster while using more positions. Plus, I'll cover ways to create even more pleasure for making both her and you feel incredible during anal sex.

.4.9 Night 7 ~
Hear those magical words you've been waiting for, "Give me more, more!"

Night 7 is exciting! Here you will see and experience a variety of positions. You will also start penetrating and thrusting more, like you do with vaginal sex. Plan to set up ahead of time to create the mood, include music and lighting. Enjoy implementing the necessary techniques from Nights 1–6 to get her ready for the pleasure you will both experience. Prepare and clean all the toys you will use. Use different toys to stimulate her. Use the silicone beads and/or the Spectra Beaded Anal Vibe for her stimulation. Then you can use the Spectra Gels Anal Toy to get her ready for anal sex.

If your woman can cum multiple times, you can give her an orgasm before you begin anal sex to relax her. If your woman has one or two intense orgasms, then build up the excitement but hold off on making her cum until you and she are engaged in anal sex. At the edge of the bed, start in the missionary position again to build intimacy. Once you have followed the techniques in Night 6 to enter her gem, grab your cock and lift it up so you are providing more stimulation to the G-spot area. Stroke it

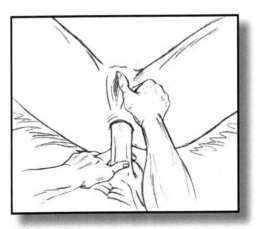

in and out while providing this upward stimulation. Since you are at the edge of the bed, kneel so you can angle the head of your cock upward, and you'll be able to deliver even stronger stimulation. Now you are both properly angled, and you can lift your cock with your hand to stimulate her G-Spot [See Image 4.24].

4.24

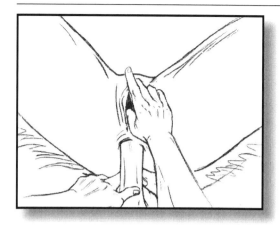

Get feedback from her to see if it feels good to her and what angle and pressure she prefers. Push your cock downward and see if it is pleasurable. Try different angles and more pressure to the sides, and see what feels good to her. Indulge in the things she enjoys. Remember to keep clitoral stimulation on her

4.25

at all times with a toy or your fingers. Insert your thumb in her pussy to massage her G-Spot and the soft side of your first and middle fingers to massage her U-Spot and clitoris [**See Image 4.25**].

Apply a good amount of lube to help keep the stimulation slippery and wet. Have her hold a toy for now, since vibrations provide powerful stimulation.

You can now bring her legs to the very edge of the bed, so her ass is at the edge as well. Try the different angles in her gem by manipulating your knees and hips. Continue to grab your cock to pull up, push down, pull side to side, and do circles as you stroke in and out to see what she likes. Massage her pussy with one hand while the other massages the area around her gem, as your cock slides in and out. If she likes it rougher, pull her hair back, bring her up, and passionately bite her neck. Play with her nipples and turn her head to engage in passionate kisses as you thrust into her beautiful and tight gem! If she

4.26

likes her nipples squeezed or having your hand erotically around her neck, then do so. Engage in passionate, hot, and dirty talk to enhance the excitement.

Now you are going to change positions. Grab one of her ankles and lift her leg, so her foot is pointing to the ceiling [See Image 4.26]. Enjoy this for a bit, and then put her legs to the side, so she is now on her side. This position enables you to enter at different angles; try a variety of angles, and especially try angles that will stimulate her G-Spot. Use your hands to stimulate her pussy, her perineal sponge, G-Spot, labia, and clitoris. Spank her if she likes it because spanking releases endorphins of heightened arousal. This position and doggy style are great for spanking.

Become a master of the psychological and biophysical factors of arousal. Do outer gem and pussy massage as you are going in and out of her gem. Spread her ass cheeks to give you more access to this area [See Image 4.27].

Excite her both physically and emotionally throughout the entire experience. In the beginning, it is especially important that you continue stimulating her clitoris and other erogenous zones while engaging in anal sex. You should always provide stimulation, but when she is accustomed to anal sex, you can use both hands to give her stimulation in other ways. Put both hands on her nipples, or one hand touching her lips while the other is massaging her G-Spot.

4.27

You can do all the positions you would do in normal intercourse, and for every new position apply more lube. Make sure you go in slowly, ensuring that the angle is okay for her. Use the vibrator on her clitoris to enhance stimulation when entering her in a new position. There are certain positions where you can use your pelvic bone to provide the clitoral stimulation.

For example, if she rides you while facing you, put lots of lube on your pelvic bone area and lots of lube on her clitoris and pelvic area. Position a small pillow under your butt to lift your pelvic bone a little higher. When she is sitting on you, she can angle her upper body so that her clitoris is being massaged against your pelvic bone as she moves back and forth. You can join in the movement as long as the rhythm is pleasurable for her. She can lay her breasts on your chest and move to stimulate her clitoris while you are in her gem. Kiss her passionately, and with her heart next to yours, imagine your souls becoming one in that moment. Use your hands to spread her ass cheeks.

Put your hands on her waist to move her around. Then, pull her in closer to your pelvic area. Reach around and massage the outside of the gem sensually, and use your fingers as follows:

Right hand:

1. Use your pinky and ring fingers to massage and play with her gem ring and tang.

2. Use your first and middle fingers to massage the back side of her gem ring.

Left hand:

1. Use your first and middle fingers to massage the other side of her gem

2. Use your ring and pinky fingers to massage her pussy and her clitoris (designate these fingers for pussy play only, and do not use the gem play fingers for playing with her pussy) [See Image 4.28].

Now you can start engaging in a variety of positions. Use toys, plugs, and vibrators in her gem while you are in her pussy. Or use the toy in her pussy while you are in her gem (but remember, never insert anything used the gem in her pussy). The 7 Nights to Ecstasy is a detailed system that defines how to take it slow, and it is a baseline, but it may have to vary depending on the man's size and the woman's specific anatomy. Depending on your size, you may need to redo Night 5 more than once, even several times, so you can gradually accustom her to something closer to your size before you go in her gem. Some women may be able to go a little faster through the nights—but, let them guide you. It's better to take your time because if you mess up or go too fast and you hurt her, you will most likely bring a stop to the whole process.

It will be hard for her to regain trust in you when it comes to anal sex. Do not mess up and create a situation where you need to ask for forgiveness. Put yourself in her shoes: How would you like it if she got revenge on your butt by doing what you did to her? I'm sure your butt is clenching up right now.

Yep, mine is just from writing about it. So don't mess up on her. Take all the time that she needs since it is all about pleasure anyway. As I stated earlier, you can now start trying out the different positions that you do during vaginal intercourse. You will also be able to add to them. In the next chapter, I am going to describe a variety of positions and strategies that you can use to enhance stimulation the anal sexuality and add variety to your new found erotic pleasure.

4.28

Chapter Summary

Chapter Four ~ Seduction Philosophy ~

Enjoy the Process of Pleasuring Her, and Give Her Thrilling Orgasms Every Little Step of the Way

4.1 Body Seduction

    a. The strategy to lead her from curiosity to fulfillment, or from NO to Oh My God that was AMAZING, is to convince her body so that her mind follows, by leading her body through the first, small steps.

4.2 Patience is Pleasure

    a. The 7 Nights to Ecstasy is a baseline measurement. Depending on your size and your woman's anatomy, it may take longer. No matter how long it takes, it's all good because you will enjoy the process.

    b. In the 7 Nights you are only going to go as far as she feels good. Continue to pleasure her with the activities she likes to do and that make her feel incredible. If you do these things for as long as she likes, she'll start to enjoy a little bit more.

    c. REMEMBER: IF YOU GO TOO FAST AND GET TOO EAGER, YOU MIGHT END UP HURTING HER. IF THE TRUST IS GONE, THE RIDE WILL PROBABLY BE OVER! SO TAKE THE TIME TO ENJOY THE RIDE!

4.3 Set-up Ahead of Time to Be Smooth During

a. As you progress through the steps you will need toys and lubes. Instead of going back and forth into drawers and closets, have all your tools of the trade set-up ahead of time.

b. Presentation is important. Get a cool box or bag that you can easily access. Keep it next to you when you are pleasuring your woman.

c. Cleanse each other and check yourselves right before sex; ensure you both smell and taste good.

4.4 The Process In Detail, Nights 3 to 7 ~

How to perform every touch, lick, and caress

a. If your woman sees this book, she'll discover it is designed to entice her to want to try the system for the pleasures she will enjoy.

4.5 Night 3 ~ Triple her pleasure

a. Start with the techniques of Nights 1 and 2 to arouse her. Express and experience the erotic art of your souls together (read the second paragraph of Night 3).

b. You are going to lick her clitoris as you slide your middle finger in her pussy to massage her G-Spot. Lubricate her gem well and play around her gem area. Then slide your pinky finger to the first knuckle, pause, allowing her to get more relaxed and comfortable. After she has adjusted then continue.

c. Using the Circling Technique, go to the second knuckle. Let her relax and feel comfortable before you go farther. All of this is happening while you are simultaneously licking her clitoris and massaging her G-Spot.

d. Slide two fingers into her pussy so you can cover a larger area of her G-Spot or massage her G-Spot with one finger and her perineal sponge with the other finger. Continue to lick her clitoris.

e. Review the illustrations of Night 3. After you use your pinky finger to play with her, do the same process again. This time use your middle finger. Make sure you reapply lubricant.

f. You can use the V-Spot Massage Technique and the CrissCross Technique, as covered in chapter 5.

g. SEPOR – get lost in this moment, and you will reach the O and then perform the R.

4.6 *Night 4 ~ Vibrate her soul*

a. Start with the techniques of Nights 1 and 3 to arouse her. During this night you are going to insert a vibrating toy with slightly bigger girth than your finger into her gem.

b. You are going to lick her clitoris as you slide your middle finger in her pussy to massage her G-Spot. Lubricate her gem and have the Vibrating Plug or The Tingle Tip ready.

c. Before playing with her gem, use the vibrator to play on her clitoris and play around her pussy. Inside her pussy, stimulate her G-Spot and perineal sponge.

d. Use the **Circling Technique** to enter her gem with a vibrating toy.

e. Slow down when you get to a girth that is bigger than your middle finger, because that is where she left off. Go slower at this point, using Circling, and pausing every half-inch to let her get used to the girth and enjoy the pleasure from all the stimulation. She will then enjoy you going farther inside of her.

f. Use the **oooh OOOHs Technique** to enter her gem with the base vibrator from the dilator set. Let her relax and feel comfortable before you go farther inside of her. All this should happen while you are simultaneously licking her clitoris and massaging her G-Spot.

g. Slide two fingers into her pussy, so you can cover a larger area of her G-Spot, or massage her G-Spot with one finger and her perineal sponge with the other finger. Continue to lick her clitoris.

h. Review again Night 4's illustrations. After you play with her using the base vibrator, put on the first attachment from the dilator set. Reapply lubricant and use the Circling oooh OOOHs Technique.

i. Perform the V-Spot Massage Technique, as covered in chapter 5.

j. SEPOR – get lost in this moment and you will reach the O, and then perform the R.

4.7 Night 5 ~ Expand her ecstasy

a. Start with the techniques of Nights 1 and 4 to arouse her. During this night you are going to insert a vibrating toy with bigger girth that is closer to the girth of your cock.

b. You are going to lick her clitoris as you slide your middle finger into her pussy to massage her G-Spot. Lubricate her gem and, after playing with the Vibrating Plug or The Tingle Tip, get ready to use the Berman Dilator Toy with the first additional attachment, as you did on Night 4.

c. Before playing with her gem, use the vibrator to play on her clitoris and play around her pussy. Inside her pussy, stimulate her G-Spot and perineal sponge. Use **the Circling, oooh OOOHs and Pleasure Twists Techniques** to enter her gem with the Berman Dilator vibrating toy. Have her enjoy this while you lick her clitoris and massage her G-Spot.

d. Put on the second attachment to the Berman Dilator and do as item (c.) above. But this time slow down because this is a new, bigger girth than she has had before.

e. Additional variations include using a pussy vibrator on her clitoris as you enter her gem with the Berman Dilator. You can use a G-Spot vibrator as well. If you are well endowed, you should redo Night 5 again on another night with a toy that is closer to your girth. On a different night, put on the third/last attachment to the Berman Dilator and do as item (c.) directs. Go slow with the Circling oooh OOOHs Technique.

f. Other fun activities during Night 5 are the Good Vibes position and the U-Spot Love technique covered in "Erotic Play and Positions That Will Stimulate Both of You in Amazing Ways."

4.8 Night 6 ~ Entering the gem of intimacy

a. Start with the techniques of Nights 1 thru 5 to arouse her. On this night you are going to insert your cock into her beautiful gem.

b. You are going to lick her clitoris as you slide your middle finger inside her pussy to massage her G-Spot. Lubricate her gem. And after playing with a Vibrating Plug, **Use the Leave in Technique.**

c. Lubricate her clitoris, pussy, U-Sport, around her pussy, and gem. Stimulate all of her with your cock using the illustrations provided throughout Night 6.

d. Use the **Waves of Lubrication Technique** to thoroughly lubricate her gem, so she can take you inside smoothly.

e. Use **Circling, oooh OOOHs, and Pleasure Twists** along with a vibrator on her clitoris. Ask her how she is feeling as you start to go inside of her. If she says she feels tight, use the **Gem Relax Technique,** and then start pleasuring her again.

f. Use the oooh OOOHs Technique and pause at every inch to let her get adjusted. Wait for about 30 seconds or so. Tell her that you are going to pause and when she is comfortable, to let you know by saying "YESSS", then you will continue. Keep using the Circling, oooh OOOHs, and Pleasure Twists to progress the pleasure forward. Reapply lubricant at every inch, to make sure she is fully lubricated. Review the **5 Steps to Enter Her Gem.**

g. Look into her eyes, kiss her, tell her how beautiful she is, how sexy she is, and how good she feels. Enjoy every moment and don't think about how far you can go inside. Think about thoroughly enjoying and pleasuring her at that exact moment. Get lost in that moment, and the experience will progress naturally.

h. If you have a big or bigger cock than the toys you have been using, be considerate to her. She trusts you with her gem, and you need to treasure it. Keep the focus on her pleasure and your enjoyment of pleasuring her. Don't try to pump her hard and fast right now; that will come in time. You will have her cumming and cumming from that soon enough if you progress with patience.

i. Once you are halfway or more inside, put lubricant on her and your pelvic area. Lean down to have your chest close or next to her breasts. Position a vibrator on her clitoris so it continues stimulating her. As you go inside farther, take one hand and put it behind her neck. Look into her eyes. Let her know how good she feels and how gorgeous she is, and kiss her with all your passion. The intimacy created the first time you enter her gem is very deep.

j. Use slow and sensual movements. Night 7 is when you will use more positions and engage in harder thrusting. You want her to enjoy this time and not be sore afterwards. Enjoy the intimacy for a while. Implement the SEPOR method at the end and give her an orgasm. Give her a purposeful break at 20 minutes to a half-hour or so, then ask how she feels. Night 7 is just around the corner, and you two will have even more fun then.

4.9 Night 7 ~ Hear those magical words you've been waiting for, "Give me more, more!"

a. Start with the techniques of Nights 1 and 6 to arouse her. On this night you are going to insert your cock into her beautiful gem.

b. You are now in her gem, and she is on her back on the edge of the bed. Angle your cock in different positions to stimulate her G-Spot and her other erogenous areas.

c. Get feedback as to which directional pressure she likes. Continue to simultaneously stimulate her clitoris.

d. Lift one of her legs up, and angle her to the side. Then, put both of her legs together to one side. Use your hands to stimulate her pussy, perineal sponge, G-Spot, labia, and clitoris.

e. Heighten her endorphins by spanking her (if she likes that; if not, my book Erotic Flow will cover expanding sexual boundaries). Play with her nipples, caress her body, and hold her neck as you kiss her. Talk dirty and/or passionately, or whatever turns you two on.

f. Put both of her feet on the floor, or have her kneel, and go inside doggy style. Continue to have her hold the vibrator on her clitoris.

g. Ask her what speed and deepness feels best to her. Do that only; do not mess up and thrust inside of her more than what you have gotten her used to.

You don't want to mess up now after all the time you put in. You will be able to go deeper and faster soon enough, if you are able to do it carefully and listen to her now.

h. Remember not to place toys, fingers, your cock or anything in her pussy after they have been in her gem.

i. You can do practically any position that you do in vaginal sex when having anal sex. In the next chapter, I cover anal sexuality techniques that I enjoy the most and that are different from those described in other books on the market.

Chapter Five
Erotic Anal Play

Delicious Stimulation for Both of You

5.1 Erotic AZ Play and Advanced Positions

Now that she is enjoying anal sexuality, you two can begin to diversify your new-found delight. In the following pages I provide erotic anal play techniques and positions, fun from A to Z. Toys are also incorporated to heighten pleasure for her and for you. You will use simultaneous stimulation to make her feel incredible and angle your cock so you stimulate her G-Spot while you are in her gem. Remember to include passionate, hot, erotic talk before, during, and after. Find the words and phrases that turn both of you on. Women, use your hands to pleasure yourself and him too. Take an active role in giving and receiving pleasure with the way you move, your moans, your words, facial expresions, and your flow with your lover. Both of you should view it as a mutal work of art. Every time you engage, you are going to create a beautiful masterpiece of emotions, passion, sensual creativity, erotic variety, and hot intensity—painting amazing images/experiences that will stay in your memories forever. The following techniques will add delicious excitement and fulfillment to anal sexuality. Pay special attention to the finger stimulation techniques.

a. The E3

The E3 is about stimulating her to ecstasy at three points, her clitoris, inside her pussy, and her gem. You will need to have a lubricant next to

you on the bed. Have her lay on her back in the middle of the bed—you will need to have at least a full size bed. Then position yourself somewhat perpendicular to her while laying sideways on your left side (if you happen to be right-handed) [**See Image 5.1**].

5.1

Here are the details: Play with her first and use the head of your cock to play with her clitoris, her lips, and around her gem. On a large bed, lay her in the middle on her back with her head on the pillows at the top of the bed. If you are right-handed, lay on your left side. Then you are going to play with her delicious pussy with your cock before you enter her. Pour lubricant on your hands, her clitoris, pussy, and gem. Now lift your body and her ass so that your left-hand lubricated fingers can play with her gem, while your right hand focuses on stimulating her clitoris and her pussy [**See Image 5.2**].

Now, you will start thrusting inside of her, waving your body, circling your hips, going in and out while you are simultaneously stimulating her

5.2

clitoris, pussy, and gem. Sensually enter her gem with the middle finger of your left hand and go in slowly, as deep as possible but so it's still comfortable for her.

This is a great way to stimulate her in all three places. Then she can reach down and put her hands on your ass to pull you in deeper. Now she can enjoy you thrusting inside her pussy with your cock, your right hand stimulating her clitoris and lips, and your left-hand fingers inside her gem. Mmmmm!

After she is accustomed to one finger in her gem, slide two fingers into her gem using the same technique [**See Image 5.3**]. A variation of E3 is once she is enjoying anal sex, slide your cock into her gem and use one hand to massage her G-Spot with you middle and ring fingers and massage her clitoris with your thumb. With your other hand massage around her gem ring sensually, as you slide your cock in and out of her gem.

5.3

b. Palms of Pleasure

In this position you will play with her warm, wet, and delicious pussy, while you go inside her warm, inviting gem.

Left hand: Lubricate and massage the area around your cock and in between her gem and pussy while you go in and out.

1. Use your first and middle fingers to massage her gem ring and her tang.

2. Use your ring and pinky fingers to massage the back side of her gem ring.

Right hand: Lubricate her clitoris and pussy generously.

1. Insert your middle and ring fingers into her wet pussy. Curl your fingers so that they massage her G-Spot, and use your palm to stimulate her very slippery and lubricated clitoris and U-Spot. Massage her clitoris with your palm sensually as you go in and out of her pussy with your fingers.

2. Use your first finger and pinky fingers to massage her labia as you go in and out of her sweetness.

Lick and bite her shoulders. Suck her tongue, kiss her passionately, and talk dirty to each other. Imagine that you are sending your erotic energy to your palm, fingers, and cock. Keep massaging her clitoris and U-Spot in circles, side to side, up and down, faster and slower, and not with the intent of making her cum, but with all your passion to pleasure her. Ask her what movement she likes the most. Do that movement, and she will probably have an incredible orgasm squeezing her gem around your cock and pulsating around your fingers [See Image 5.4].

Palms of Pleasure variation: have her lay down along the edge of the bed. Lubricate her well. Use one hand for palm-massaging her clitoris, and insert your middle and ring fingers into her sweetness. Then use your other hand to insert your first finger on top of your middle finger into her gem. Then use your thumb to massage her tang as you go in and out of her gem. Since you are standing on her side, you can slide your cock side to side on your pelvic area

5.4

c. The V-Spot Massage

This licking technique is VERY pleasurable for your woman. I call it the V-Spot Massage because you will be massaging her pussy from the bottom up in a V-type movement, and from top down in an upside down V movement "∧". This requires some multi-tasking on your part. By the end of this book, you will have become an erotic, multi-tasking master, who can give her pleasure in multiple erogenous zones simultaneously, and not only physically, but in mind, body, and soul as well. The V-Spot licking technique starts by lubing her gem, pussy, clitoris, and all around her pussy. Since I am right-handed, I will describe the act using my own dominant hand. Lay her on the edge of your bed, so you have room to move around and have leverage when standing or kneeling on the floor.

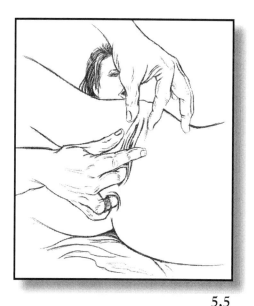

5.5

1. Insert your ring finger into her gem, slowly and sensually. After some play you can also insert your pinky at the same time.

2. Insert your middle finger into her pussy and massage her G-spot and perineal sponge. Refer back to image 4.1

3. Use your thumb and first finger to massage the outside of her pussy (her labia) creating a V-shaped motion **[See Image 5.5]**.

4. Take your other hand and do a similar action, coming down from the top of her clitoris to the sides of her pussy. Play with her clitoris and massage it with your thumb and finger like you are stroking her off.

5. Lick, suck, and kiss her clitoris, her pussy, around her pussy, and her legs, while you are doing the finger technique described above **[See Image 5.6]**. Sensually massage her labia and clitoris into your lips, suck and lick her with all your passion.

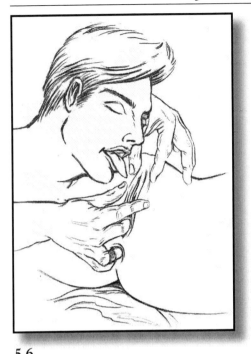

5.6

6. Talk sexy to her, tell her how beautiful she tastes, feels, and looks. Talk dirty, hum and moan passionately on her clitoris and pussy. Send all your energy and passion to your tongue, fingers, and lips.

7. Move your right hand in and out so your ring finger is going in and out of her gem while your other fingers are massaging her pussy.

Switch stimulation by moving your top hand to stimulate her nipples. Kiss and lick her stomach while your hand is still moving back and forth. Do so sensually and at varying speeds. Use your first finger from the same hand to stimulate her clitoris, while your other hand is on her breasts and nipples, and your mouth is switching to multiple erogenous zones and back to her clitoris.

d. The V-Spot Massage and Vibe Combo

The V-Spot massage is very pleasurable, and this technique also helps her become adjusted to allowing a bigger girth inside her gem. You are going to use a vibrator and/or the Vibrating Plug in her gem while giving her the pleasure of the V-Spot massage.

1. Insert the Vibrating Plug and hold it with the area of your palm below your pinky and ring fingers. Insert the toy into her gem, slowly and sensually. Use your fingers and palm to guide the vibrating plug back and forth as you implement all the techniques of the V-Spot massage. [See Image 5.7]

2. You can also use the Berman Dilator Set. Attach the first or second additional attachment to the base toy. Insert the toy in her gem slowly and sensually. Then, put your pinky and ring fingers on the back of the

toy to control the in and out action.

3. Insert your middle finger of the same hand into her pussy and massage her perineal sponge.

4. Use your thumb finger and first finger to massage the sides of her pussy and her lips.

5. Use your other hand's thumb and fingers to massage the clitoris. Implement all the other aspects of the V-Spot massage.

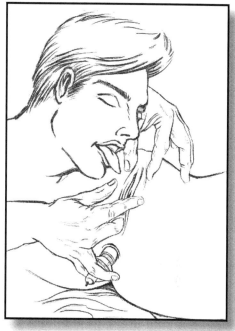

5.7

Use both the V-Spot massage and the Vibe Combo to bring her to orgasm, so she continues to associate lots of pleasure with anal play. It is important not to focus only on getting her to orgasm. Just get lost in the moment with her, and indulge in the pleasuring of her. Let her feel that all your passion and energy are being sent to her in every lick, kiss, suck, and caress. When you have no goal, when you both get lost in the moment and in each other, when you just enjoy it for its erotic beauty, and enjoy the bliss of amazing pleasure you two are experiencing, she will tend to orgasm for you. She wants to feel your heart and soul. She will be more excited than ever when she sees how turned on you are from experiencing that pleasure together, and the orgasm will come.

e. *Missionary Work* ~
It's all about giving

While you are in a very intimate missionary position as you are going into her gem, reach around with one or both hands and massage the area around her gem sensually.

Left or right hand:

1. Use your first finger to massage the back of her gem ring.

2. Your middle finger massages the area in between her gem and her pussy, the tang area.

3. As the ring finger plays with her clitoris, kiss her passionately, bite into her neck and shoulder while massaging, and sensually slide in and out of her warm gem. Massage her, putting sensual synchronization into your strokes.

5.8

4. Use your fingers to massage all around her gem. Slide your middle finger across her tang as you thrust deep inside of her gem.

5. Use your other hand to stimulate her other erogenous zones [See Image 5.8].

5.9

Also, in Intercourse Missionary Work, reach around to massage all the areas mentioned above.

Right or left hand:

1. Insert your first finger into her gem.

2. Your middle finger is playing with her tang.

3. Your ring finger is on the other side of your cock, playing with her clitoris as you are thrusting in and out of her pussy.

You can also insert two or more fingers inside her gem. Play with the area around her pussy, clitoris, and tang. It is quite a delight to see her enjoying the hot intimacy of this move because you two are so close together [See Image 5.9].

f. Tongue Tingle

While she is still on her back, and you are performing Night 2 and licking her gem, make sure you penetrate it with your tongue as much as you can, slowly. Once you are as deep as you can be, curve your tongue up.

Now insert your middle finger into her pussy. Curve the finger down, so you can massage your tongue, which is in her gem, with your finger inside her pussy. Circle your finger(s) around your tongue. Massage it in many ways, and then exchange your finger for a

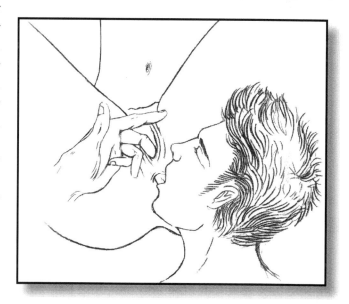

5.10

toy, and massage your tongue, which is deep inside her gem. Curve down the vibrating toy to vibrate your tongue and up to massage her G-Spot. Then try this again in a 69 position. Penetrate her pussy with your tongue, as deep as you can, to curve your tongue up and massage your tongue with your finger in her gem or a toy, like in Position X – Bottoms Up [See Image 5.10].

9. *Pleasure Twists*

This technique is important in the beginning and very pleasurable for her even when she is used to anal play.

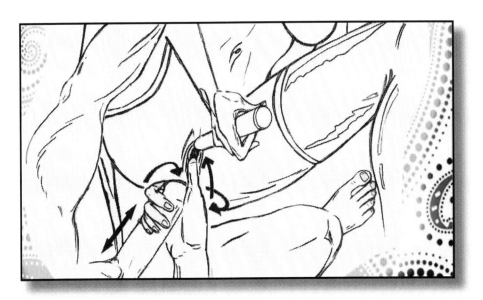

5.11

1. As you start to put the head of your cock inside her gem, bring your dominant hand to the head and put your fingers around your it. Make sure they are all well lubricated. Sensually twist your fingers around your cock's head so the side of your first finger to the bottom of your thumb can massage the area around her gem.

2. As you twist, your thumb slides in and out of her pussy, massaging her tang and perineal sponge.

3. As you are doing this, grab your shaft and enter her slowly, **use Circling** to get her adjusted to your width. Keep massaging and twisting your fingers around her ring as you enter her gem more deeply. Use small circles as you enter or push downward on your cock, see which she likes.

4. Take your other hand and massage her clitoris or nipples, switch back and forth.

5. Move back and forth, side to side, and wave your body inside her gem while doing all the above.

Yes, it requires multi-tasking, but what a fun endeavor! The pleasure she will experience from the entering process will significantly increase because the ring area has many nerve endings. Do more of whatever she likes. Continue until you are fully inside, and do it while you are going in and out of her beautiful gem [See Image 5.11].

h. The CrissCross

Sensually, get into a 69 position, you on the bottom. Lick her thighs. Lick across erotically from one side of her pussy to the other. Kiss her clitoris sensually and passionately; lick it slightly; kiss it; suck it. Then you are going to insert the middle finger of your left hand into her pussy, and the middle finger of your right hand into her gem. Move your fingers in and out while making a massaging motion with your fingers. The left-hand middle finger will be massaging her G-Spot.

Now, you are going to start sucking her clitoris, wrapping your lips around with the tip of your tongue waving, and massaging the tip of her clitoris. Feel all your energy come to your mouth, lips, and tongue. Feel your heart and soul concentrated in your tongue and lips. Generate the sense of how it feels right before you are going to cum. Now imagine sending that intense feeling and energy to her clitoris. As you do this, you are going pull down the finger that is inserted in her gem, and push up the finger that is in her pussy. The fingers will CrissCross [See Image 5.12].

Slightly wave them, move them to the CrissCross position slowly—to make sure she is enjoying it— and in that moment. Suck her clitoris as if your mouth were cumming from sucking her so passionately. Moan with pleasure; moan with vibration, so that your throat

5.12

generates vibration, that resonates on your lips. Whatever she and you hear is very stimulating, give her ear candy while you are sucking her. Lick with so much passion that it feels as if you were cumming by doing that to her. She will enjoy the finger technique combined with the pleasurable sucking.

i. The Straddle and Flip

While you are on your back at the top of the bed, have her straddle your face, with her hands on the wall or on the bed frame, and with her wet clitoris and lips over your mouth. Start by kissing, licking, and biting her

inner thighs. Then work your way towards the center, circling your tongue and taking light to deep sensual bites of her. As you get close to her lips, slow down, and glide your tongue across her lips lightly in order to glaze her with the wetness of your passion. Make sure your tongue is really wet, and make your tongue warmer by breathing warm

5.13

breaths into your mouth.

That way, when you go near her lips, she will relish how warm and wet your tongue is, making her warm and wet as well. After pleasuring her clitoris and pussy, have her tilt her gem, so you can lick it sensually and passionately [See Image 5.13].

Enjoy her soft gem over your tongue. Have her spread her knees, so more of her gem is flush up against your tongue, so more of her pussy is flush against your mouth, so her wetness is all over your mouth. Then put your

5.14

hands on her torso and push her back, so she rolls back on the bed onto her shoulders, and her ass rolls up to face the ceiling [See Images 5.14 & 5.15].

Her knees are going to be by her ears; her shoulders, on the bed; and her back is going to be supported by your torso. Your legs are spread, and you are sitting upright. In this position you have full access to her gem in a very hot position. Begin to lick her softly, and then more passionately. Lick her pussy and her clitoris. Then lick her gem while you massage her clitoris with your fingers.

Right hand:

1. Your first finger massages the back side of her gem while your tongue licks her gem.

2. Your middle finger massages the inner ring of her gem. Ring finger massages her tang and bottom of her pussy.

4. Your pinky finger massages the labia.

5.15

Left hand:

1. Your first finger massages around your tongue, licking her gem. 2. You middle and ring fingers massage her pussy and inside, the perineal sponge.

5.16

3. Your pinky massages her clitoris [**See Image 5.15**].

You can add toys to this play. Use one hand to hold the toy and play with her clitoris and the inside of her pussy. You can use the side of your hand to twist the toy and massage her labia and clitoris. Use your other hand to spread her ass cheeks apart and lick as deeply as you can into her gem. Have her spread her ass with her hands, so you can lick her gem deeply, and thrust your tongue in and out of her gem [**See Image 5.16**].

j. Good Vibes

I call this next move "Good Vibes" in support of the store Good Vibrations for providing a professional, cool, and educational atmosphere to teach people about sexuality. This is one of my favorite anal play positions with a toy. Once your woman likes anal toy play, you can engage in this act. So, after you have warmed her up for anal play, get a chair, preferably an office chair that drops low, swivels around, and has no arms. Drop the chair to its lowest position. Have her straddle you, and enter her pussy. Use the head of your cock to play with her pussy before you enter. Now you can use a vibrator with either a stopper or a cord that goes around your wrist, or another system to ensure the vibrator does not go all the way in and disappears inside her gem.

Lubricate her soft, warm gem, the vibrator, her clitoris, and your pelvic area, so her clitoris slides on you when she rides you. First, play with the tip of the vibrator on her gem. Then slowly start to insert the vibrator in her gem. Once you are inside, hold the vibrator still for a little bit so you both feel the vibrations. The vibrations will be felt through the thin wall between her ass and pussy, and it is going to feel incredible for both of you. Go in and out, then in circles with the vibe. By tilting the vibe away from her body, it will angle to the front towards your cock. This is the definition of good vibrations. Mmmm, mmmm, good vibes! Use your fingers to add stimulation:

Right hand:

1. Your first finger massages the back side of her gem ring around the vibrator.

2. Your middle finger massages the inside gem ring.

3. Your ring finger massages the tang.

4. Your pinky massages her clitoris. You can also do this with your ring finger.

Left hand:

1. Holds the vibrator while circling it and twisting it.

2. Use the side of your hand that is against her skin to massage her gem ring by twisting the vibrator when it is deeper inside her gem [**See Image 5.17**].

Both of you will most likely explode from this play. You can also switch positions by using a more pliable toy, like the Spectra Gels Anal Toy with a vibrator option. Ensure that it is fully clean, and then put in her pussy. Position the plug stopper vertically on top of her clitoris so that it is more stimulating for her clitoris, or horizontally if it is more comfortable. After the plug is comfortably in, you can enter her gem with your cock and enjoy!

5.17

k. Pearls

After she has been thoroughly stimulated from both regular sex and anal play, and before she cums, use a pearl necklace or silicone beads to massage her ass. Then push the pearls into her gem. Get pearls in a couple of different sizes to see which she likes best.

Put in as many as she feels comfortable with. Then, continue to have normal intercourse. Have her tell you when she is about to cum, so you can pull out all the pearls as she is cumming. Pull them out at a speed that will enable her to enjoy the grooves of the pearls coming out of her gem. Not too fast. Ask her afterwards what speed she likes, so you know exactly how to make it feel the best for her. Always clean your toys thoroughly after play. To cleanse the pearls for use at another time, put them into boiling water. To make sure the pearl string doesn't break easily, test its strength before you insert it into her [**See Image 5.18**].

5.18

l. Fingertips

During this type of anal play, you will want to her on her back. You are going to arouse her as usual. Then, after some finger play, you are going to lick her hot, wet pussy and clitoris. Then you will slowly guide your middle finger into her gem or you can slide both first and middle fingers inside.

Next, sensually guide your thumb into her pussy. Touch the fingertip of your thumb to your middle finger while you're inside her gem. Start to massage your fingers in circles, side to side, and in and out. Continue to lick her clitoris while you are doing this. Use your other hand to stimulate both of her nipples. Have her lick your fingers to get them wet and ready for touching her. You can also pull out your thumb and insert two fingers

5.19

from your other hand into her pussy. Then turn them over horizontally to play with and massage the finger or fingers in her gem. Trace the outlines of your fingers massaging her inner sugar walls [**See Image 5.19**].

m. *Eyes Wide Shut*

Once she is comfortable with anal play on her back, then you can start bending her over, which provides a beautiful view. For this position, you are going to need a blindfold, lubricant, toys, and a chair. Now that your woman is accustomed to anal play, this experience will be even more erotic for her. First, start with her on the edge of your bed, facing the bed. Pull her hair back and lick her neck; bite into the area between her neck and shoulders [**See Image 5.20**].

Kiss her passionately, and begin to lick her back and the back of her neck. Now you will blindfold her, heightening her other senses. Continue to lick her back, and circle your tongue all the way down to the small of her back [**See Image 5.21**].

Stay there for a bit, and then continue down to her ass cheeks; where you will take soft, sensuous bites of her cheeks. Continue down the back of her leg, then to the back of her calves, and down to her ankles. Come back up and over her inner thighs and lick across her wetness. Go down the other side and repeat this process. Then, come back up her other inner thigh for

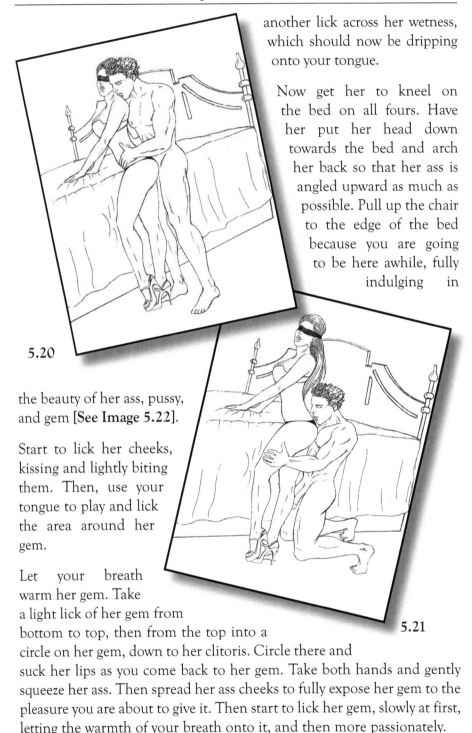

another lick across her wetness, which should now be dripping onto your tongue.

Now get her to kneel on the bed on all fours. Have her put her head down towards the bed and arch her back so that her ass is angled upward as much as possible. Pull up the chair to the edge of the bed because you are going to be here awhile, fully indulging in

5.20

the beauty of her ass, pussy, and gem [See Image 5.22].

Start to lick her cheeks, kissing and lightly biting them. Then, use your tongue to play and lick the area around her gem.

Let your breath warm her gem. Take a light lick of her gem from bottom to top, then from the top into a

5.21

circle on her gem, down to her clitoris. Circle there and suck her lips as you come back to her gem. Take both hands and gently squeeze her ass. Then spread her ass cheeks to fully expose her gem to the pleasure you are about to give it. Then start to lick her gem, slowly at first, letting the warmth of your breath onto it, and then more passionately.

Then, have her reach back to spread her ass cheeks for you, so she can join the erotic play. This frees you up to start playing with her pussy. Gently circle and slowly slide your warm tongue into her gem. Go as sensually and deep as you can while she spreads her ass cheeks for you. Meanwhile, play with her clitoris. You can also slide two fingers into her pussy and slide the vibrator into her gem. This is just

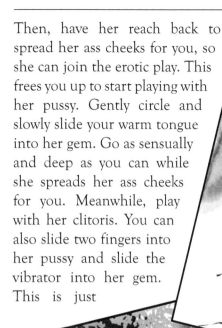

5.22

like when she was laying on her back, but now she is bent over with the triple stimulation of your tongue in her gem or around her gem ring while a vibrator is inside, your fingers in her pussy and you're playing with her clitoris.

5.23

After you both enjoy this play for awhile, stand up and enter her pussy with your cock. Use the Slim Vibe vibrator to play around and inside of her gem. Use the fingers of your free hand to massage her ring area around your the Slim Vibe sliding in and out of her gem. After enjoying this, you can pull out and use another toy to insert into her pussy, while your cock goes inside her gem.

Use a different Slim Vibe vibrator to play around and inside her pussy. Now use the fingers of your free hand to massage her ring area around your cock sliding in and out of her gem [**See Image 5.23**].

You can continue to use a variety of toys to stimulate her. Remember to lubricate the toys and not to go from her gem to her pussy with these toys. This position is delightful to look at. You can let her enjoy the vision by taking a picture or a video from your perspective and showing it to her later. She can delete it afterwards if she wants, but it is a great way to share your visual experience with her.

n. Upside Down Gem Spot

This position is famous in the adult film industry. I am going to add some technique to what you have probably already seen. This is a very visually stimulating position for both of you. You can do this position at the edge of the bed or the couch. You should have toys, a lubricant, a camera, and extra-soft pillows. There are several ways to enter and perform this position. First, we will start with the bed method. Put several pillows on the floor near the edge of the bed.

Sit on the edge of the bed and have her straddle you with her legs extended out on the bed.

Lean her back, support her back with your arms. Let her head drop until her shoulders land on top of the pillows on the floor [**See Image 5.24**]. Make sure she is comfortable. Play with her clitoris, pussy, and gem with the head of your cock. Get her really wet, and lubricate her gem. You can now enter her gem slowly. Use a vibrator on her clitoris as you enter. You are now standing over her gem in a slightly crouched position. First, enjoy going up and down in this position. After some play, let yourself get as hard as you can. You are going to use the stiffness of your cock and some geometry to angle the head of your cock to stimulate her G-Spot through her ass.

Right hand:

1. Middle and ring fingers on her clitoris.

2. First finger stimulates her pussy lips and inside her pussy.

3. Thumb massages the circumference of her gem.

Left hand:

1. First and middle fingers massage her tang.

2. Thumb massages circumference of gem on back side of your cock.

3. Ring finger on her labia.

Once you are hard, lean back. You might need to slide the top mattress back somewhat from the box spring, so it gives you room to move back and forth and down and around. Your cock will now be angled in her gem to stimulate the upper walls of her pussy and her G-Spot. You might need to push her slightly forward to get it right. Move up and down as well as back and forth to see what feels best to her. Make finding her G-Spot pleasurable. Once you find the area, move around to have your cock's head massage the spot sensually and erotically. You will be playing with her clitoris and pussy simultaneously. Now start to switch your foot position and begin turning around gradually. If she is at a 12 o'clock position, move to the 10:30 position. Now fuck and play in this position. Then, go to a 9 o'clock position, and fuck in this position. Switch to 7:30, and fuck in that position. Then switch to 6 o'clock. In this position, you can bend over more. Have her play with your gem as you enter deeply into

5.24

hers. Slap her ass, massage her ass. Use your fingers to massage her gem ring as you slide in and out. Do the same for the rest of the way as you did to get to 6 o'clock, until you go full circle [**See Image 5.25**].

You can also have her lay on the bed on her stomach and have her upper torso slide off the bed, so her hands and elbows are on the floor. Face the bed and help her flip her legs towards you so you can enter her gem from this position while you play with her clitoris.

Another version of this position is very exciting, but it requires your woman to be somewhat acrobatic. You stand with your back to the wall. She stands several feet away from you, facing you. She then does a handstand right in front of you. You catch her legs while she maintains the handstand in front of you. She is now upside down with her face and torso facing away from you. Angle her gem towards you, as you let her legs curve back. This will angle her ass perfectly in line with your cock. Then you can enter her gem while she is still in the handstand position.

5.25

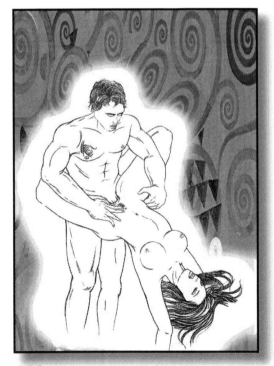

5.26

This position is exciting to see and do. You can then angle yourself to massage her G-Spot with the head of your cock through her ass. Use your fingers to massage her tang, pussy and clitoris [**See Image 5.26**]. If you want to keep the loving on the bed, you can do the same position with you sitting on the bed and your woman lying in front of you [**See Image 5.27**].

5.27

o. Gem 69

This is another pleasurable position for both of you. You can do this while she's on her back, both of you on your sides, or while you're on your back. Have toys and lubricant ready and nearby. Having your woman lick your gem feels really good. You can both enjoy the pleasure provided by a warm wet tongue on your gem. Make sure your hygiene preparation is as good as when she did it in order to make it pleasurable for her, too. This means shaving your ass! You don't want to lick a really hairy ass, and neither does she. More importantly, you will feel a lot more of her tongue when you are shaved. You should also cleanse the way she does with antibacterial soap and your pinky finger going inside of you. Then, start by licking her pussy and move to include her ass. She starts at your cock, then to your balls, and licks until you both "end up" in gem 69. You can use toys to add to both your pleasures.

p. Upside Down V-Lick

Have her go on the bed and assume a kneeling, bent-over position. Have her put her breasts as close to the bed as possible. Then, have her arch her back as much as possible, so her gem is facing up. Next, she should reach back with both hands to grab each butt cheek and slowly spread her gem for you to indulge and lick freely. First, slide your middle finger into her pussy and curve it up. After some erotic licking, sensually and passionately slide your tongue deep into her gem, so you can feel your tongue with your finger inside her pussy.

After massaging your tongue and finger for a bit, put both your first finger and your middle finger into her pussy. Curve both up and make a slight V-shape with your fingers and pull back, so that your tongue goes in even deeper and lick between the V created by your fingers. Massage your fingers with your tongue, and your tongue with your fingers, in a variety of ways. Pulling back and forth towards your tongue helps your soft, warm tongue move in and out to stimulate her gem deeply, as she spreads herself for you.

While she's in this kneeling doggy position, you will do a V-Spot massage. Lubricate her clitoris, pussy area, and gem area.

Right hand:

1. Insert your middle finger into her pussy and curve it down to massage her G-Spot.

2. Extend your first finger and ring finger up to massage around her gem while you are sliding in and out of her pussy.

Left hand:

1. Come down from the top of her ass to her gem with the bottom of your middle finger facing her gem and massage her gem sensually.

2. Slide your middle finger into her gem and extend out your first and ring fingers to massage the sides of her pussy.

You now have two hands at play, with the middle finger of each hand facing one another. The bottom hand's middle finger is in her pussy while the first and ring fingers massage the area around the gem. Use the palm of this hand to stimulate her clitoris as you slide your finger in and out of her pussy. Simultaneously, the other hand will be sliding its middle finger in and out of her gem, with the first and ring fingers massaging her V-Spot area (the area just outside her pussy lips), and your mouth will go wherever it can find room to kiss, suck, bite, and lick her deliciously.

g. Ride-Em

You have the option of many positions you can try once your woman has gone through all 7 Nights and is comfortable with anal sex. You can do practically everything that is possible with normal sex (depending on your size and how comfortable it feels to her in different positions). Although, with anal sex, there are some interesting dynamics and angles that add pleasure in these positions. Have all your fun tools ready for easy access. You may need a small pillow for this Ride-Em position. To start, let her take the top position. An adjustable incline weight bench is great for this position, but not necessary. Of course, this is a favorite in normal intercourse, but I will provide some techniques to add even more pleasure for the woman experiencing anal sex in this position.

First, make sure you have trimmed your pubic hair to a short level with clippers or scissors; the shorter, the better. Have her straddle you after you have stimulated her. Put lubricant all over her ass, pussy, clitoris, and the area above her clitoris. Then, put lubricant all over your cock, your balls, the area above your cock, and your entire pelvic area. Enter her gem while massaging it as you go in. Have her lay her breasts on your chest.

Her pussy and lips will now be placed flush against your pelvic bone area, and since you are in her gem, her clitoris will be higher and right around your pelvic bone. Since you both are fully lubed, have her slide up and slowly go down while gently moving her hips around. The slippery effect of the lubricant allows her to slide up and down easily. Now, have her clitoris slide up and down on your pelvic bone. Play with direction, and tilt your pelvic bone higher to stimulate her. Try putting a small pillow under your ass and back to lift your pelvic area higher. Pour more lubricant on her gem. Use both hands to sensually massage her ass and her gem, which is now wrapped around your cock. Squeeze her ass; squeeze it together, then spread it.

Shake each of her ass cheeks in opposite directions and in the same direction, fast and at varying speeds. The shaking creates vibration and adds stimulation. Add more lube and have your fingers trace the circle of her gem sensually and passionately. This serves two purposes: first, it adds stimulation to her gem. Second, it keeps your cock and her gem well lubricated while you are sliding in, out, and all around. Reach around and massage the outside of the gem sensually. Use your fingers as follows:

Right hand:

1. Use your pinky and middle finger to massage and play with her gem ring and tang.

2. Use your first and middle fingers to massage the back side of her gem ring.

Left hand:

1. Use your first and middle fingers to massage the other side of her gem.

2. Use your ring and pinky fingers to massage her pussy and her clitoris (designate these fingers for pussy play only. Do not use the gem play fingers for playing with her pussy).

Many times all that stimulation at once will make your woman have an explosive orgasm while you're in her gem [See Image 5.28].

Another variation is to have her lean back and support herself with her hands on

5.28

the bed. As she leans back, have her slide back, so the head of your hard cock is now angled to massage her top vaginal walls through her gem.

Now you can massage her G-Spot with your cock through her gem. Wave your body sensually to stimulate her G-Spot. Enjoy!

r. Ride Him On All Fours

Use a couch for this position. You lay on the floor with the back of your knees, calves, and feet on a couch. She then will stand over you at the edge of the couch while you face each other. Lift your butt up as high as possible and she will squat down so you slide in her gem. You then will use the couch as leverage for your legs to thrust up. She will put her hands on the couch for support and use the strength of her arms to do squats up and down. She can squat to an ideal position so you can thrust up and down for her pleasure and you can hold a level position so she can slide up and down for your pleasure. Use your fingers to add stimulation:

5.29

Right hand:

1. Use your thumb and/or fingers on her clitoris and U-Spot. Also, use your thumb to play with her G-Spot, while your fingers play with her clitoris.

Left hand:

1. Use your thumb to massage the ring of her gem and her tang.

2. Use other fingers to play with her labia, the inside of her pussy, and her perineal sponge.

Regardless of who is moving, it's all pleasurable for both and the view is delightful [See Image 5.29].

s. G&G

G&G stands for gem and G-Spot. Before getting into this position, have your lube ready and next to you on your bed. Once you have done all the arousal play and have started anal sex, lay her on her back on the edge of your bed. You are going to be standing at the edge of the bed. Lubricate her gem, clitoris, and pussy. You are going to use the sensual entry technique of small circles and thumb play, as explained earlier, to enter her gem. Once you are in her gem with your cock, you're going to move to the side a bit so you can use your right-hand to enter her pussy.

Right hand:

1. Slide your middle finger (and first finger if she likes two fingers) into her pussy. Curve up your fingers to stimulate her G-Spot.

2. With your fingers inside her pussy, massage her U-Spot and labia with your thumb.

Left hand:

1. Use your thumb and first finger to massage and stroke her clitoris.

2. Switch and use your middle and ring fingers to massage from the top of her clitoris down to her labia.

Lick your left fingers, give her clitoris a light slap, and then massage it sensually. You can use a toy, or you can have her use a toy, to stimulate her clitoris as you play with her nipples.

Massage her G-Spot, sending passion to your fingers. Circle her G-Spot and all around her pussy. You can also use a G-Spot toy to insert into

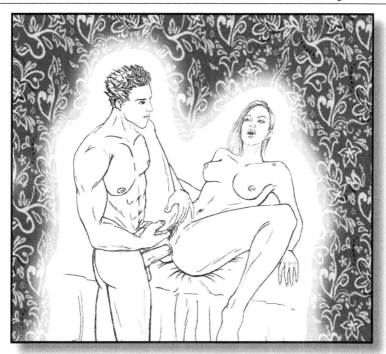

5.30

her, instead of your fingers. You have many options to stimulate these designated areas. You also have a good view of your hard cock entering her beautiful gem, as her wet sweet lips are spread for you, and her clitoris is full [See Image 5.30].

Another stimulating option used in this position is to insert your thumb inside her pussy, so the soft side is up. Massage her G-Spot, and with her clitoris well lubricated, massage her clitoris with the palm area under your fingers.

You can also insert your cock into her pussy, but remember that if you have already been in her gem, you need to change condoms. Then use your fingers to play with her gem. It's just like Image 5.30, except your cock will be in her pussy. Your left hand will be in the same position, and the right hand will pleasure the gem in a couple of ways. First, you can insert your middle finger into her gem while your thumb plays with her U-Spot. Second, you can insert two or more fingers into her gem deeply while your thumb plays with the area between your cock and her gem. She will enjoy the double penetration from the heat of your hands and your cock. You both will probably orgasm from how good this feels. Another way to angle your cock to massage her G-Spot through her gem is to position her gem at the edge of the bed and instead of moving back and forth in her gem, let your knees drop down so your cock is angled directly up and will be massaging her G-Spot on the way back up. Keep moving down and back up sensually. This also works if you are in her pussy. While in her pussy, if you put a pillow below her ass you can angle yourself to reach her cul-de-sac, an arousal zone illustrated in image 4.1. Experiment with different angles to reach and stimulate this erogenous zone that can lead to lots of pleasure for her.

t. Reverse Cowgirl Massage

In the Reverse Cowgirl position, your cock will be in your cowgirl's gem. You are going to have her lay back on your chest. You are going to reach around with both hands.

5.31

Right hand:

1. Put the first and middle fingers across and above her gem, to massage her tang.

2. The ring finger and pinky finger go below your cock, to massage the backside gem area.

Left hand:

1. Use your ring finger and pinky finger to play with the inside of her pussy.

2. Use your first and middle fingers to massage her clitoris.

Do not switch hands once you have started. Keep the gem massage hand on the gem area, and the pussy massage hand on the pussy [See **Image 5.31**].

u. *Bend Over, Beautiful*

A great way to provide pleasure is to have her in a doggy-style position. Go into her pussy with your cock (remember, wash thoroughly if you are entering after anal sex, or switch rubbers), and insert your middle finger inside her gem, and curve it down, so that

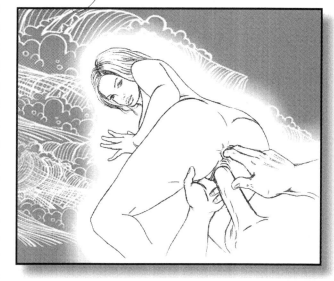

5.32

you are applying pressure on top of your cock and pushing your cock more towards her G-Spot through her gem, and/or you can massage her

middle wall against your cock. With your other hand, use the tips of your first and middle fingers to massage her clitoris, labia, and tang. You can insert the middle finger, or more fingers inside her gem, depending on what turns her on [See **Image 5.32**].

Other stimulation during doggy-style is to insert your thumb in her gem. Insert the thumb facing down and massage the top of your cock and around. Then reach down with your fingers to massage her clitoris while

5.33

your cock is thrusting inside her pussy. Use your free hand to stimulate other areas (breasts, lips). Also, insert your thumb facing up and massage the upper walls.

You can doggy style inside her gem. Insert your cock into her gem and use one hand to play with her clitoris and pussy. Turn your palm up and use your fingers to play with her clitoris and U-Spot. Also, insert your thumb in her pussy to play with her G-Spot. Additionally, insert your fingers in her pussy to play with her perineal sponge, while the other hand stimulates her gem area around your cock, or her nipples [See Image 5.33]. She can then reach in-between her legs to massage your balls as you slide in and out.

v. Naughty Butterfly

The Naughty Butterfly allows you to enjoy anal sex while you stimulate her clitoris and/or G-Spot with vibration, with no hands! Tadaaa! You will be able to use your hands to stimulate other erogenous zones, and she can use her hands to arouse your erogenous zones. Since many women like anal sex with stimulation to their clitoris and G-Spot, a butterfly toy that provides only simulation to her clitoris and pussy is a good solution. Your hands are free; therefore, to massage around her gem, spank her ass, grab her waist, pull her hair, pleasure her breasts, and do the things that turn her on. She can use her hands to spread her ass cheeks, play with you, and support herself in a variety of positions. Your hands are free to support yourself in a variety of wild positions. Enjoy rough passion, or erotic play.

w. U-Spot Love

U-Spot Love is similar to the V-Spot Vibe massage, but with some differences that your woman will enjoy. Lick your woman's clitoris and all around her sweet wetness to start. Play with a vibrating plug around her gem while licking her. Insert the plug sensually until it is all the way inside, up to the stationary insertion point. Play with her perineal sponge by inserting both your ring finger and middle fingers in her wetness. Then, play deeper inside of her and massage her A-Spot. Use your thumb and first finger (same hand) to squeeze her lips sensually on the outside of her U-Spot. Massage her U-Spot from the sides at the same time your other

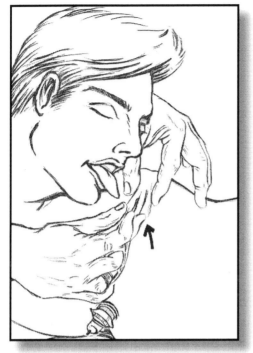

hand's thumb and first finger are massaging her clitoris, and lick her as well. Have her enjoy this for a bit. Then use the first finger from the hand that has the two fingers in her pussy to massage the U-Spot directly.

Your finger will be below her clitoris but above or to the sides of her urinary hole. Massage the U-Spot with small circles and apply a little bit of pressure. Ask her what feels best. Get feedback, so you know exactly what pressure she likes. Once you know, then suck her clitoris with all your soul, heart, and passionate energy. At the same time, massage her clitoris with

5.34

the other hand, suck her clitoris, massage her U-Spot, massage her G-Spot with your middle finger, and massage her perineal sponge with your ring finger, all while a vibrating plug stimulates her gem! I know it sounds like a lot to think about, but practicing will result in so much pleasure—she will love it **[See Image 5.34]**!

k. Bottoms Up

Have her lay on her back, and get in a 69 position. Most guys will concentrate on the clitoris and on licking the lips. This technique does that but goes beyond typical licking. Definitely do start with the sensual and passionate licking of her clitoris and her pussy. Add stimulation to her pussy with one hand and to her gem with the other. Make your tongue stiffer and lick her U-Spot.

Now you are going to lick down to the bottom area of her pussy. Turn your head, so you are angled to where your lips are about the same direction as her lips. Take one side of her labia at the bottom of her pussy. Start sucking it into your mouth, sensually and slowly. As you do this, suck

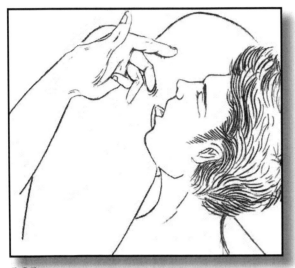

her into your mouth as if she is your favorite dessert, one you have not tasted for years. Suck her bottom labia passionately and deeply into your mouth. Go as deep as you can with your tongue into the bottom of her pussy. Send all your energy to her labia, as though it is coming from your heart and soul. While you are doing this, you are also

5.35

playing with her gem [**See Image 5.35**].

Then move your mouth to the center-bottom of her pussy, lick the bottom inner wall of her wetness as deeply and as passionately as you have ever licked. Explore the bottom wall with your tongue sensually. Moan and groan in the pleasure of what you are experiencing together. Then, slowly move to the other side to suck her labia deeply into your mouth, just as you did the first side of her labia. As you finger her gem with one or two fingers, sensually lick her tang and the edge of her gem ring. Since you are in a 69 position, she can be pleasuring you, too, using both hands to pleasure you while she sucks.

y. Body Quake

Lay her on her side and place her butt at the edge of the bed facing out, and her breasts facing towards the inside of the bed. Place a power massager, like the Hitachi Magic Wand Massager, on her clitoris and U-Spot. Slide your cock into her pussy and fuck her sensually. Then slide another vibrator into her gem. You can move the vibrator inside her gem in an alternate movements opposite to your thrusting or in the same motion. The power of the Hitachi-type massager will give her an orgasm that will shake the earth below you.

Your neighbors will be very jealous of her [**See Image 5.36**]! You can switch it up and slide your cock into her gem, and use a new or thoroughly-washed vibrator in her pussy while the power massager is on her clitoris. She can also hold one or both toys while you use your hands and fingers to stimulate her in other erogenous zones.

5.36

z. *Hand Quake*

Another variation of the Body Quake can be done without vibrators, and you can use your hands. Use the same position, or you can do this in a spooning position, too. Lubricate her everywhere and very well. Slide your cock into her pussy, use one hand to play with her clitoris and U-Spot, and slide two fingers into her gem. Stroke your cock and fingers at the same time, in and out, and then alternate with your cock in, and your fingers pulling back. Depending on the position you are in, see if you can do anything with your mouth, like licking her body or fingers, and engage in HOT sex talk. This can achieve an anal orgasm, a G-Spot/pussy orgasm, and a clitoral orgasm all at the same time! It is amazing to see, hear, and enjoy this beautiful event!

Another version of the Hand Quake is after she is used to a lot of anal penetration, grab the base of your cock while you are in her gem. Circle your cock around and/or move it up and down and side to side fast and vigorously while you play whith her clitoris. Adjust to the speed and intensity to what she likes best.

5.2 Waves of Variety

There are many positions that you can use when you want ecstasy through anal sex; the possibilities are immense. The key is that when you are introducing her to new positions, you want to make sure it feels good for her. It should be something that you both are enjoying. You want to make sure you are creating an intimate and erotic moment. Plus, you want to experience amazing sex. You should make sure you pleasure her well enough to warm her up to any new positions you want to introduce. Use the vibrator on her clitoris to help aid a pleasurable entry, and massage her gem during anal sex, so you are stimulating the area and keeping it well lubed, at all times.

When introducing her to new positions, be conscious always to stimulate all her senses, her clitoris, G-Spot, U-Spot, A-Spot, and gem, and most of all, her mind, body, and soul. This will enable her to try and enjoy a variety of different positions. For more information about creating delicious erotic experiences and having amazing sex, check out my other book *Erotic Flow*, which will go deep into those topics. An overview is provided in section 5.5 and on EroticFlow.com. This book is meant to provide you with the information you need to know in order to move a woman from never trying anal sex, or who is scared of it, to loving it and having amazing orgasms from anal sexuality.

5.3 Exercises ~
Consistently enhance the experience

There are things your lover can do to help the process when you two are not together. How often you see each other will determine whether she might need to engage in gem play on her own. If you two have sex with each other two to three times a week, then you might not need her to do her own gem play. But if you see each other once a week or less, then too much time might be passing by between gem play opportunities for consistent progress to be made. Once you have taken her to the point of Night 3, when she is enjoying your finger, tongue, and plugs in her gem, she can engage in masturbation with a finger, plug, or other toy to maintain the progress you two have made together.

Your woman can use the Berman Dilator set, the Juli Ashton Beginners kit, The Tingle Tip, and any other toys she likes. It's good practice to begin with a shower or bath and doing an anal flush. Then, she can set up the mood that turns her on, including lighting and music (see section 5.5). The strategy here is for the woman to stimulate herself, and then play with a smaller plug at first and work up to bigger sizes. She can leave in a plug while she plays with her sweet pussy and clitoris, so that her gem gets used to the size. Women, remember to stimulate your clitoris as you put the toy or plug inside your gem.

If you are in a monogamous relationship, I advise not using a toy that is much bigger than your man. Stay within the size range you two have already tried together, so that her gem gets conditioned to enjoying her specific man, so he can still feel her gem snug around him. You want to provide a lot of stimulation when increasing sizes. It is better to experience this together than the woman by herself. It is a very erotic experience to increase the size that she can take inside her gem with her partner. This builds intimacy and it associates the experience of sexual exploration with her partner. Also, it is good to go up in size after you have licked her gem so good that she cannot wait to get more. She should be yearning for more of your experience and exploration together.

Have her try masturbation while laying on her back, or by bending over and reaching around. Depending on how comfortable she is with pictures and videos, she can make you a video of herself masturbating with gem play, which would be a highly erotic turn on—mmm, mmm. Chapter 8 of the book *Anal Pleasure and Health* by Jack Morin, PhD, does a good job of explaining scientifically the biophysical response of anal masturbation. Also Google "female anal masterbation." If there is hesitation, you will find answers to any questions you may have.

5.4 Ever-Evolving Pleasure

This book was written with the woman in mind, to introduce her to a new world of sexual delights with anal play and anal sex. The intent is to provide a pleasurable process to get her there. If you complete the path laid out in this book, you will have more than doubled the variety of things you can do sexually by enjoying the arousal and ecstasy of anal play. So this method is designed to seduce her body and her mind simultaneously throughout the process. By making her body feel incredible, having her mind follow the process of small steps, connecting intimately, and rewarding her with amazing orgasms along the way, you should be able to condition her to enjoy the process fully and not have it ever be painful. You must communicate together along the way, and build trust by letting her know that if she feels any pain, you will slow down or stop, give her a rest, and try again later or at another time. Never try to push too quickly, because if she experiences a lot of pain at any point, it will be hard to have her try to go past that point ever again.

Just put yourself in her shoes—you would want your partner to be considerate of your pain thresholds. If she ever says slow down or stop, then do so and let her know how much you appreciate her and her sensuality for exploring with you. Kiss her passionately, and make sure she does not feel that you are upset or frustrated. If you are following my method, know that it is a delicious sexual experience all along the way. It won't hurt, and it will be filled with pleasure. Once she begins enjoying anal sex with deep penetration by your cock, she will cum in new ways. She and you will find many new methods, acts, and positions that will make both of you explode. Once she is comfortable with anal sex, you can start each time in different ways, and open up a new erogenous zone for toy play.

Gem/anal sex and play is also a great way for women who have recently given birth to enjoy an erotic sexual experience while recovering from the birth process or if it is that time of the month and they do not want to have vaginal sex. Some people use it to finish a sexual session so the guy cums in her gem and therefore not risk pregnancy. Though not 100% effective, if sperm happens to slide out of her gem onto her pussy.

5.5 Erotic Flow

This is a sensual, intimate, passionate, fun, and erotic journey. To continue along this path, read more about the erotic seduction of her mind, body, and soul. Get my book *Erotic Flow - The Art of Seducing the Mind, Body, and Soul.* - 2011 release. Pre-order at EroticFlow.com.

Erotic Flow – Seduce the Mind, Body, and Soul Overview:

Seducing Her Mind and Body:

1. Seducing the mind – creativity, spontaneity, sensuality, intimacy, wildness, animalistic passion, erotic fantasy, and love.

2. Seducing all of her senses – what she sees, hears, smells, tastes, and feels.

3. Seducing her body – lips, tongue, cheeks, neck, legs, breasts, thighs, calves, feet, toes, stomach, back, small of back, pelvic bone, and pussy area (surrounding area, labia, clitoris, tang, ass, ass cheeks, U-Spot, G-Spot, A-Spot, perineal sponge, and cul-de-sac).

Seducing her soul:

1. Flowing Together – Becoming One – Getting lost in the moment, nothing else exists, you are fully engulfed in the experience of each other.

2. Cultivating Erotic Energy and Exciting the Soul – How to create powerful erotic energy from your heart and soul, and send it to your lips, tongue, hands, fingers, and erogenous zones. Hence, enabling you to give deep captivating pleasure to your lover's mind, body, and soul.

Erotic Flow:

1. Discovering and expanding your lover's sexual boundaries.

2. Enjoying the full range of experience from erotic sensuality to rough animalistic passion.

3. Designing creative erotic experiences and fantasies, that will leave you grinning for a lifetime.

4. Creating moments when you and your lover's passion, energy, and soul become one. Moments when you become lost in each other, when nothing else exists, except the intense, deep, and delicious connection with your lover.

Chapter Summary

❧❧

Chapter Five ~ Erotic Anal Play ~

Delicious Stimulation for Both of You

5.1 Erotic AZ Play and Advanced Positions

The following summaries give a quick description of the type of sexual act involved in each activity.

a. **The E3** - Intercourse sex with simultaneous stimulation to the clitoris, pussy, and gem, while in a cross position.

b. **Palms of Pleasure** - While inside her gem, you massage the area around her gem with one hand, lubricate her pussy area, insert your middle and ring finger into her pussy, and massage her clitoris.

c. **The V-Spot Massage** - This is a pussy-licking technique that pleasures the clitoris, the exterior and of the interior pussy, and the gem.

d. **The V-Spot Massage and Vibe Combo** - This is a pussy-licking and vibrator technique that pleasures the clitoris, the exterior and interior pussy, and her gem.

e. **Missionary Work... It's All About Giving** - In a missionary position, while going inside of her gem reach around with one or both hands and massage the area around her gem, in between her pussy and her gem, and her clitoris. Also during intercourse in the missionary position, reach around to massage the same area, but also insert your finger or fingers inside her gem. Play around her pussy and tang.

f. **Tongue Tingle** – A gem-licking technique that stimulates the gem and pussy.

g. **Pleasure Twists** – A gem-entry technique to help her enjoy the entry process.

h. **The CrissCross** – A clitoris-sucking and pussy-pleasuring technique.

i. **The Straddle and Flip** – A pussy, gem-licking, and vibrator technique that delivers lots of excitement.

j. **Good Vibes** – An intercourse and gem sex technique with lots of vibrating stimulation to her and you.

k. **Pearls** – A gem-play and pussy-licking technique that adds pearls or silicone beads to accentuate pleasure.

l. **Fingertips** – A gem-, pussy-, and clitoris-play technique with which you will massage her inner walls for stimulation.

m. **Eyes wide Shut** – A fantasy technique to stimulate her whole body, arouse her senses, and thoroughly pleasure her gem.

n. **Upside Down Gem Spot** – An anal sex position that includes more pleasuring techniques than the typical porno scene.

o. **Gem 69** – Exactly what it sounds like; it is how to enjoy you licking her gem while she licks yours.

p. **Upside down V-Lick** – A deep gem-licking technique to put the warmth of your tongue into her beauty as deeply as possible. Also a way to do the V-Spot Massage in the upside down position.

q. **Ride-Em** – Anal sex technique, so she can have an anal and clitoral orgasm from riding you through pelvic stimulation.

r. **Ride-Him On All Fours** - An anal sex activity that enables her and you lots of freedom to thrust.

s. **G&G** - This activity stands for gem and G-Spot. This position will give her G-Spot stimulation while you are in her gem with your cock.

t. **Reverse Cowgirl Massage** - A hot position where the girl straddles you facing away from you. Add the finger techniques provided for stimulation to greatly enhance her excitement.

u. **Bend Over Beautiful** - Another way to pleasure her, is to have her in doggy style position, go in her pussy with your cock (remember, wash thoroughly if it is after anal sex, or switch rubbers), insert a finger or two in her gem, while you massage her clitoris with other fingers. You can also insert your thumb in her gem and move it in different directions.

v. **Naughty Butterfly** - Since many women like anal sex with stimulation to their clitoris and G-Spot, a butterfly toy that has only simulation to her clitoris and pussy is a good solution. Your hands are free; therefore, you can still massage around her gem, spank her ass, grab her waist, pull her hair, pleasure her breasts, and do the things that turn her on.

w. **U-Spot Love** - Insert a Vibrating Plug sensually until it is all the way in to the stationary insertion point. Play with her perineal sponge by inserting your ring finger and middle finger in her wetness. Then play deeper inside and massage her A-Spot. Use your thumb and first finger from the same hand to squeeze her lip sensually on the outside of her U-Spot. Massage her U-Spot directly.

x. **Bottoms Up** - Lick to the bottom area of her pussy. Suck her bottom labia deeply, and then lick the bottom of her pussy deeply.

y. **Body Quake** - With her ass at the edge of the bed. Use a powerful Hitachi type massager on her clitoris, insert your cock in her pussy, and another vibrator in her gem. Another option with clean toys: insert your cock in her gem and the vibrator in her pussy while the power massager is on her clitoris.

z. **Hand Quake** - Variation of the Body Quake can be done without the vibrators, and you can use your hands.

5.2 *Waves of Variety*

To introduce her to a variety of anal sex positions, make sure you are always stimulating all her senses and multiple erogenous zones: her clitoris, G-Spot, U-Spot, A-Spot, Cul-de-sac, labia and gem, but most of all her mind, body (all over), and soul.

5.3 *Exercises ~ Consistently enhance the experience*

If you only have sex with your woman once a week or less, you will need her to practice her own anal play in-between your together sessions, so she does not lose the progress made during those sessions. If she plays at the level where you left off at least once, preferably twice a week, she will maintain more of the progress with you during your together sessions.

5.4 *Ever-Evolving Pleasure*

You now have more than doubled your sexual knowledge and the variety of positions available to you. Just to re-cap the pleasure process: seduce her body and mind simultaneously throughout the process. If you ever proceed at a pace that is not comfortable for her, stop and let her adjust, and only do what is pleasurable for her; do this so well until she is yearning for more. Gem play and sexuality is also a great way for couples to have sex after the woman gives birth.

5.5 *Erotic Flow*

This is a sensual, intimate, passionate, fun, and erotic journey. To continue along this path and read Erotic Flow, Seduce the Mind, Body, and Soul get my book *Erotic Flow*. The book covers the following:

a. The erotic seduction of all her senses – what she sees, tastes, smells, hears, and feels both physically and emotionally.

b. **How to flow in the moment,** so that you and your woman become one by losing yourselves in the moment.

c. **How to cultivate and send erotic energy to any part of your body,** so you can enhance the experience of flow.

d. How to **create delicious, erotic experiences** to delight each other always with new, exciting fantasies. Also, **discover and expand her sensual and erotic realms of experience!**

Resources

Alan P. Braur M.D. and Donna J. Brauer *The New Promise of Pleasure for Couples ESO: How you and your lover can give each other hours of Extended Sexual Orgasm* © 1983

Bill Strong with Lori Gammon, *Anal Sex for Couples: A Guaranteed Guide to Painless Pleasure* © 2006

Cathy Winks and Anne Semans, *The Good Vibrations Guide to Sex* © 2002

Coralie Trinh Thi, *Dare to Have Anal Sex: Saucy Sex Advice from France* © 2009 U.S. Translation

Don Miguel Ruiz, *The Mastery of Love: A Practical Guide to the Art of Relationship* © 1999

Dudley Seth Danoff, M.D., F.A.C.S., Superpotency: *How to Get It, Use It, and Maintain It for a Lifetime* © 1993

Eric Fromm, *The Art of Loving,* © 1956

Eve Eschner Hogan, M.A. with Steve Hogan, *Intellectual Foreplay: Questions for Lovers & Lovers-to-be* © 2000

Graham Masterton, *How to Drive Your Woman Wild in Bed* © 1987

Jack Morin, Ph.D., *Anal Pleasure and Health: A Guide for Men and Women* 3rd edition, © 2008

Jack Morin, *The Erotic Mind: Unlocking the Inner Sources of Sexual Passion and Fulfillment* © 1995

Kerry and Diane Riley, *Tantric Secrets for Men: What Every Woman Will Want Her Man to Know About Enhancing Sexual Ecstasy* © 2002

Kim Powers, *Turning Her on to Anal-Sex* © 2005 Denmark

Lonnie Garfield Barbach PH.D., *For Yourself: The Fulfillment of Female Sexuality* © 1975

Mantak and Maneewan Chia, Douglas Abrams, and Rachel Carlton Abrams-M.D., *The Multi-Orgasmic Couple: How Couples Can Dramatically Enhance Their Pleasure, Intimacy, and Health* © 2000

Michael Morgenstern, *How to Make Love to a Woman* © 1982

Nina Hartley with I.S. Levine, *Nina Hartley's Guide to Total Sex* © 2006

Sindy St. James and Cindy St. James, *How to Get Her to Watch Porn, Have Anal Sex, and Call Her Best Friend for a Threesome* © 2008

Susan and Clyde Hendrick, *Liking, Loving, and Relating* © 1991

Tristan Taormino, *The Anal Sex Position Guide: Best Positions for Easy, Exciting, Mind-blowing Pleasure* © 2009

Tristan Taormino, *The Ultimate Guide to Anal Sex for Women* 2nd edition, © 2006

Some competing books above are provided so you can compare this book versus other books on the market for the introduction phase of anal sex and the detail of the advanced positions chapter.

Website Resources and Author's Bio

On the EroticFlow.com website you will find the author's bio in the About EF section and have access to a variety of different resources to enhance the learning experience as well as make it entertaining. Visit the website for promotions available to owners of this book. In the members area, there will be video tutorials, DVDs, and discounts on EF fashion, toys, products, and services.

Videos

Women have stated that they need to see a woman having pleasure from anal sexuality in order to believe it. I have collected a variety of videos on the Internet of women having intense orgasms from anal sex. In the members area, I provide links to these videos, so women and men can see how good they can feel from anal sexuality. I also provide recommendations to the best anal videos portraying women who are thoroughly enjoying anal sex.

Film Stars

There are adult film stars that are amazing at showing how incredibly pleasurable anal sexuality can be as well as great techniques you can use during anal sex. In this section I highlight the best anal adult film stars so that couples can look for their DVDs and videos. You will enjoy the HOT sexual experience they share on screen, and I will provide comments on what makes them great.

Toys

This will be a continually-updated section for the best toys for introducing a woman to anal play and erotic sexuality. Advanced toys are also highlighted with reviews.

Music

Many times couples do not have the time to select the best music to set the mood for a hot and passionate encounter with their lover. It takes time to look for the best music, to sequence it right, to set up music that will deliver a specific vibe that you want, so you two can flow together just right. Whether you want the vibe to be sensual, passionate, romantic, erotic, or a combination, it takes a lot of time to have a large collection to keep things new and exciting. I have done the work for you! I have been collecting music to enhance the experience of flow since 1992. This section will enable you to enjoy streaming music that is a compilation of years of music to seduce your soul. It is ear candy for delicious sessions with your lover. You will able to buy any of the streaming songs. I will also have mixed CDs for specific vibes that you can purchase on the site.

Clothing

This section will feature clothing designed by Erotic Flow and other designers. You will see uniquely HOT tops, shorts, lingerie, caps, and accessories for purchase. If you are famous or have a large following of people on the Internet, contact EroticFlow.com for the Promo Program (Code 3008) we will be providing promo EF clothing to people that can receive Promo Program benefits and EF Partners.

Facts

We are at a sexual revolution. Never in the history of time has sexuality information been so accessible for people to explore as it is today. Men can have sex until they die with the aid of Viagra, and one out of every four porn surfers is a woman. Anal sexuality between hetero couples is happening more than ever before. I posted all the research that was done for the book in this section to share the valuable research that I found in the Erotic Soul section of the site which is open to everyone.

History

Sexuality has evolved throughout history in very interesting ways. The past can teach us so much about why we are where we are. Sexuality has been cherished and repressed in different societies and times throughout history. In this section there is a very interesting history about sexuality throughout time.

Art

Erotic sexuality is the art of my soul. I love art that is an expression of the erotic soul. This section will display some of my favorite erotic art and artists on the Internet.

Photography

A photo is a beautiful moment in time captured forever! I love photography, the creative eye of photographers, and how they capture a moment in life. There are pictures that can turn you on in a second and leave an impression in your mind for a lifetime. In this section you will see some of my favorite erotic photography and photographers.

Events

This section will feature erotic events throughout the world.

Books and Audio Books

The ideas and experiences of others are extremely valuable and can provide knowledge that can change our lives. Authors pour their heart and soul into writing their books. I had to do the same for my books and the EroticFlow.com website. The online list will have comments and it will continually expand.

Consulting

For couples needing education or fantasy creation for a specific situation or event, or to address the needs of a specific situation Erotic Flow Consulting is the solution. Learn more about Erotic Flow Consulting Services on the website's link **Services**.

Webinars

For people who live far away and who would like to learn through a webinar format. There will be a presentation of the content with Q&A session so that a group of people can get specific questions answered and learn from the questions of others for a lower price than private consulting.

Social Networking

The site will provide an advanced system so that people with common interests can communicate, share ideas, and express their erotic souls.

Erotic Dialogue

This book is designed to arouse the mind of a woman. The instructions are to be implemented by her lover. I wrote the system explanations with terminology that resembles real life sexual relations. I interviewed a group of 156 individuals online. I asked how many people use the terms "vagina" and "penis" in their sex life? Do you say "lick my vagina" or "suck my penis" in your sex life? No one stated that they did. The majority of people stated those terms were not sexy.

I decided to use realistic wording that people actually use but do so in a sensual, passionate, and erotic manner. All of the explanations are about pleasuring and loving your woman. That should come across. It is the details of what and how to do things, that are the most important. If there are other words that would turn you on more, then imagine your favorite terms in place of the ones I used. The wording of the book reflects the terms of choice used by those surveyed and interested in anal sex. Everybody is different, so no matter which words I selected I would not satisfy everyone. Thus, I invite you to fantasize the scenery, the ambience, the music, the smells, the tastes, the actions, the wording, and the sensual, passionate and erotic feelings that turn you on the most to bring the explanations to life in your mind.

Anal Sex Health Research

The links below are provided to the customers of this book at EroticFlow.com/AnalSexHealth (cannot be linked to from the EF site).
http://en.wikipedia.org/wiki/anal_sex
http://healthguide.howstuffworks.com/anal-sex-dictionary.htm
http://www.sexualhealth.com/channel/view_sub/sexuality-education/anal-sex/
http://www.netdoctor.co.uk/sexandrelationships/analsex.htm

http://www.fascrs.org/physicians/education/core_subjects/2003/anatomy_colon_rectum_anus/
http://en.wikipedia.org/wiki/Anal_canal
http://www.sexhealth.org/bettersex/anal.shtml
http://www.scribd.com/doc/86887/10-Rules-of-Anal-Sex-by-Jack-Morin
http://www.ivillage.com/5-myths-anal-sex-uncovered/4-a-284083
http://en.wikipedia.org/wiki/Anal_masturbation
http://books.google.com/   (Research and preview books)

Feedback is Crucial and Rewarded

VERY IMPORTANT: Thank you for taking the time to read this book. The only way to improve the book and help other couples and women have a good experience with anal sex is to share your feedback. If you share your thoughts at **EroticFlow.com/Feedback. The site will provide you aggregate results on feedback. If for some reason you cannot visit the page, write to Feedback@EroticFlow.com.** There will be options there for you provide your opinion in order to help others. As a token of my appreciation, I will reward you by sending you bonus anal technique information. Also, a trial membership to the EF Members site when finished. No woman should go through a bad experience, your feedback and reviews will help many women not go through a bad experience and enable them to enjoy a very pleasurable, sensual, and intimate experience. What feedback to provide:

1. What you liked?
2. What needs changing (delete, less, more, or different on anything)?
3. What helped you most (sharing your story can make a huge difference)?

Share to Help

If this book provided a better experience in exploring anal sexuality, if you enjoyed some of the pleasuring techniques, or if you learned something that you think could also benefit others, then share the book with friends. You can help many women and couples not go through a bad experience(s). There are so many people that see anal sex scenes in porn videos online nowadays, that the request to have anal sex comes up more frequently than in previous decades. You can help that request turn out to be an enjoyable and intimate experience.

Let others know about the book by tweeting that you finished the book, liking the Facebook.com/EroticFlow page, or just telling a friend about it so they don't have a bad experience. If you do not want to share with your friends that you read the book, just tell them that you read an article online about it in case the topic of anal sex comes up. On the Amazon.com page or other online shop, writting a review, indicating which reviews are helpful, and clicking the LIKE button, is extremely helpful (all can be done anonymously). If you have the ability to tell a lot of people and want to make good money for doing so, read about the Partner Marketing program on the About EF page at EroticFlow.com.

Flowing is Giving

I wish you the best in your journey of passion, intimacy, and erotic ecstasy. Erotic Flow was created to help others. A portion of the proceeds from this book will go to help people in a variety of worthwhile charities in areas such as health, community development, and preservation of the environment. Read more about our giving efforts at the About EF section on the EF site. Live it to the fullest!

Spice Up Your Tech

Background resources from SkinIt.com and DecalSkin.com Visit SkinIt. com and DecalSkin.com to personalize your technology. Go through the EF site for discounts to the above sites.

Disclaimer
The information contained herein is for private informational purposes. Any facts are as timely as possible but things change. The publisher, author, editors, distributors, or booksellers do not endorse, condone, authorize, confirm, or sanction anal sexuality if it is against your religious views, or in regions of the country where the practice is illegal and are not responsible for health issues resulting from unsafe experimentation. Military couples should refer to the Uniform Code of Military Justice, Art. 125, for restrictions on sexual practices.

Acknowledgments

I am deeply grateful to my contractors, friends, girlfriend, and family, who have been instrumental in supporting my ideas, research, product creation, business development, art feedback, and promotions. Also, thank you to my friends from my high school, college, and MBA program, who helped me assess the different aspects of venturing into my own business.

Many times, alongside men who make their dreams come true, are dynamic, strong, and intelligent women, who provide support, advice, inspiration, and love. Therefore, a very deep and special thanks goes to my girlfriend who has been immensely supportive and loving. She always inspires the art of my soul and my heart. The art we create has resulted in many contributions to this book and my next book, *Erotic Flow*. Also, I am forever grateful to the beautiful women throughout my life who have inspired the art of my soul, to the special times we shared, the fun times we enjoyed, and to our friendships. Those experiences have shaped my erotic soul.

My greatest thanks go to my mother. Her love and support have been there through the best of times and the toughest of times. She is an inspiring and amazing person. Thanks to the people who have helped me come back from injury to live life to its fullest again. The success of this book will help contribute to giving back to people in need. Last but not least, I thank all the people who will become customers and hopefully friends of Erotic Flow, the company and the community we are building to create incredible life experiences.

Index

Numbers

A

B

C

Made in the USA
Lexington, KY
07 May 2011